AVID
READER
PRESS

Labor

ONE WOMAN'S WORK

Dr. Mary Fariba Afsari

Avid Reader Press

NEW YORK AMSTERDAM/ANTWERP LONDON
TORONTO SYDNEY/MELBOURNE NEW DELHI

Avid Reader Press
An Imprint of Simon & Schuster, LLC
1230 Avenue of the Americas
New York, NY 10020

First Avid Reader Press hardcover edition April 2026

AVID READER PRESS and colophon are trademarks of Simon & Schuster, LLC

Interior design by Ruth Lee-Mui

Manufactured in the United States of America

1 3 5 7 9 10 8 6 4 2

Library of Congress Control Number: 2025946786

ISBN 978-1-6680-1540-7
ISBN 978-1-6680-1542-1 (ebook)

To the unlived lives of my grandmothers, Mehry and Afsar.

And to the ob-gyns.

"Run like hell my dear, from anyone likely to put a sharp knife into the sacred, tender vision of your beautiful heart."

—Hafiz

Author's Note

While this narrative draws inspiration from real clinical experiences and patients, it is important to emphasize that all patient names and identifying details have been changed or fictionalized in accordance with ethical guidelines and regulations like the Health Insurance Portability and Accountability Act (HIPAA). Any resemblance to actual individuals is purely coincidental. The primary goal of these stories is to explore the complexities of medicine and patient care while safeguarding the privacy of those involved.

Labor

Prologue

2021

The back of a MINI Cooper Clubman, I discovered, can just barely fit a folded gynecology table with two detachable stirrups and a toolbox for supplies. For weeks I searched online for an exam table and discovered that most portable tables did not come with an option for stirrups, and most tables with stirrups came with a nod toward sexual kink. I needed an exam table small enough to fit into the back of my tiny car and light enough for me to carry into the apartments and homes of my patients.

The day before, I stood in line at the hardware store holding a square black two-by-two toolbox. The cashier chatted and smiled while she rang me up. “Aww, are you buying your husband a birthday present?”

I smiled back and nodded adoringly. “Yes,” I said. “He is going to *love* this.”

Later that afternoon I filled the box with sterile speculums, Pap smear brushes, gonorrhea/chlamydia swabs, and an IUD.

The table arrived from China six weeks after I ordered it. It came in only one color: red. Every surface was red, including the vinyl foot covers of the stirrups. Red! The color of blood and communism. The color of obstetric hemorrhages and seventh-grade periods discovered in middle-school bathrooms.

We avoided red in my profession. No red socks. No waiting-room wall art featuring red flowers. No red juju brought into spaces where women had the potential to bleed out half their entire blood volume in a matter of minutes. It was just a color, I told myself. After all, what did I expect would happen? It was 2021 and *Roe v. Wade* was the law of the land. When patients arrived at my hospital with an ectopic pregnancy, or bleeding from a miscarriage, or with threat of sepsis from a pregnancy, I had every tool at my disposal. An experienced team arrived to assist me in the operating room. Difficult, sometimes brutally painful decisions were made at the bedside. My job—to save the life of the mother, to do whatever it took to preserve the life of the baby—was as much coded into my cells as the fetal DNA I shared with my children. I was trusted, and I trusted myself and my years of training, my understanding of timelines—gestational age timing, infection spread timing, hemorrhage to death timing. I knew how to activate nurses and anesthesiologists to deliver a healthy baby via stat C-section in less than two minutes. We timed ourselves with stopwatches and I was fast.

I also knew other things—such as how to insert a camera into the abdomen, quickly suction out internal bleeding, and remove a ruptured tubal pregnancy to bring a young woman's blood pressure back up to normal range, the range required by her brain and heart to function. Or how to sit with a couple who had suffered the unexpected and rare occurrence of very premature severe preeclampsia, placental abruption, or leaking amniotic fluid that would ultimately lead to the death of the baby and, if left untreated, the mother as well.

The day the portable bed arrived, I recorded myself opening the box and removing the red table—my own private unboxing video. Looking back now, I can see how I thought I knew, but did not quite know yet, the significance. Call it instinct, call it inheritance, but after fifteen years as a physician, and after learning about Mehry, *oh Mehry*, I felt at least this: When women don't have a choice, bad things happen. When women don't have a choice, we know how their stories end.

Part One

Mermaid Hair

2018

Three of my medical assistants sit me down at the end of the day. We are in our break room surrounded by bulletin boards covered with photos from our most recent office party.

"So, we'll put half of your hair up out of the way and just work on the back half, right?" Alycia is in charge of the operation. She's lost seventy pounds over the past six months through a diet of fasting, candy, and tequila after learning her husband has another wife and family in Guatemala. This left her mascara-stained on certain days and near asleep on others. I scold her when she is down and rejoice when she is back up. She provides me with a secret drawer of Jelly Bellies, gummy bears, and strawberry bubble gum that I sneak in between patient visits.

"Right. Aqua streaks. Pops of fuchsia." I lean back in the chair. "I trust you."

The other two women bounce around the room with phones in hand. They are taking photos, posting on Snapchat and Facebook. I imagine the caption: "Giving our doctor mermaid hair!!"

A few days earlier I spent an especially pernicious bout of insomnia scrolling through pictures of women with hair dyed various shades of hot pink, turquoise, and purple. My long, brown hair has recently grown out a light-colored balayage and the ends are turning blond in the summer light. Perhaps color might ignite a spark of magic into my forty-something, doctor-mom life.

It takes about twenty minutes. The team fastens a paper sheet—the kind we use to cover naked laps during pelvic exams—across my chest. Alycia is a self-proclaimed amateur hair-and-makeup artist. She knew exactly which tubes of dye to purchase when she ran to Sally Beauty Supply over her lunch break, and now she pins up the front sections of my hair with authority. As she applies color to the long strips of hair falling around my shoulders, drips of pink and turquoise and a purplish blend of both stain the front of the paper sheet. I surrender all control. I am usually the one in charge, and right now it feels good to hand it over to her. After the color is in, the group takes a final photo. I stare at the image on the phone screen. I look like a cartoon-character version of myself, with half my hair pulled up in front and a rainbow of hair, wet and pungent, splayed across my chest.

I try to smile. This picture captures my internal midlife chaos in one unfiltered shot.

"Go straight home, Doctor A." Alycia laughs. "Hope you don't get called to the emergency room!"

The other two chime in with instructions—wait forty-five minutes, then rinse off in the shower. Use deep conditioner.

"It's gonna look great!" they call after me as I head out the door. I hear their laughter behind me and head to my car. It is well past six o'clock. I am hungry and tired and unable to stop at a grocery store looking like this. I get into the driver's seat and glance in the rearview mirror.

I look like a crazy person, I think. The summer has been one of growing anxiety. New strands of gray at my temples brought with them so many uncertainties and intimations of regret. I question my decision to become a doctor every day. Lately, I even consider leaving my career. This brings late-night panic attacks and long talks with my husband, closest friends, and not one but two therapists. For about a year now, unbeknownst to most, I have been in crisis.

"Mermaid hair." I angle the rearview mirror to point at my colored streaks. Like so many of my spontaneous ideas, it now feels frivolous and ridiculous. I wonder how quickly I can get home to wash it out before it sets.

The drive between the office and my home is the equivalent of a cleansing bath. With my days spent in total engagement with patient after patient, and the nature of my job one of unpredictable needs and heightened emotion, I relish the solitude of my twenty-minute drive home.

I turn out of the parking lot and the smell from the hair dye is profound—an attempt at floral essence to hide the strong chemical undertones. I know I am frying the bottom half of my hair with every passing minute, but fried hair is low on my list of concerns. Hair can be cut and reinvigorated in an instant. That is nothing compared to the invasive surgery I am scheduled to perform tomorrow. Or the disappointment my daughter feels when I miss her summer camp performance to deliver a baby. Or the diminishing returns my husband is certain to be feeling in our decade-plus-long marriage, where energy pours out of me all day and I require quiet and replenishment every night.

Yes, I could chop off the ends of my hair and there would be a momentary regret because, yes, I had spent the past year growing it to this long, sexy-in-her-forties length. But I know, from Deepak and Oprah and Eckhart, that everything is temporary, including the stuff that does not really matter—and also the stuff that matters most.

I am only two miles and a few minutes from the office when traffic slows ahead. I press on the brakes and roll down the windows to clear the air of dye. This slowdown is a little unusual. I creep the car forward, looking at stopped traffic on both sides. It only takes a few seconds for me to discover the reason. In the opposite lane, the side of oncoming traffic, I see a motorcycle lying sideways on the road, and next to it, the body of a woman. A quick glance around confirms—no ambulance, no fire truck, no police car. The accident just happened, and aside from a couple of bystanders hovering over the body, there are no first responders on the scene.

It is a moment doctors talk about: the instant, on the freeway, or on an airplane, when an emergency occurs and Good Samaritan laws kick in. When the request is made for a doctor to "ring their call light." A good friend of mine who is a seasoned anesthesiologist says in those moments he asks himself, "Am I a doctor? Because nobody will know if you decide you're not." I always laugh when he says this because the question of whether I am a doctor never crosses my mind in an emergency. Every other minute of the day I question my doctor-ness, but in dire situations—such as a body on the road—there is no question. Right now, I see a woman on the road and nobody around to help. I am also dressed like a person who believes she is a superhero, complete with paper cape and colored, dripping hair. I am not going to make it home for the forty-five-minute rinse and conditioner.

I stop the car and make the snap decision to rip off the paper sheet. I allow the color to simply drip, and I am aware of the matching bright-colored stains on the front of my shirt. A bystander has a 911 operator on speakerphone when I approach.

"I'm a doctor," I say quickly. "Do you know what happened?"

I speak while I move, and I move quickly. The mind-to-body connection of most physicians is quick. We can talk and move and think faster when necessary. We can observe what is right in front of us, take in our surroundings, and process multiple conversations at once. I do not know this about myself in a conscious way, only in retrospect. Thinking back to those first few minutes on the accident scene, I am acutely aware of the row of teenagers and young children on one side of the road—family members of the opposing driver. I clearly see the body-sized indent in the passenger side of the vehicle that was turning onto a driveway. I take account of the anxious, determined tone of voice of the bystander who called 911. I note a helmet flung to the side of the motorcycle—a light pink-and-gray pattern decorating the cap. And finally, I look down at the body on the road: a tiny-framed woman with long, light hair, straight down her sides. She wears jeans that I register as a size zero. *A smoker's frame*, I think immediately. A skinniness invoked by nicotine and few calories. I kneel next to her right arm and immediately feel the adrenaline leave my system. It is obvious to me that she is dead. The only color in her face is the dark-red blood frothing from her lips. Her eyes are open but fixed and gazing to the sky. I reach to check a pulse, aware that all eyes are on me and what I do next. I may not look like a doctor right now, but I just proclaimed myself as one.

"Start chest compressions," the 911 operator announces over the speakerphone being pointed toward me.

There is no pulse, and I know the futility of compressions in the moment. But children are standing on the side of the road, and a woman is holding a phone over me, and there is a body of someone's daughter under my hands. How old is she? I think this several times and cannot tell. There is no color to her hair or skin to indicate. She could be thirty or seventy and it does not matter. I clasp hand over hand, find her sternum, and begin compressions.

"*One, two, three . . .*" The woman on the other side of the body counts my compressions in a loud, firm voice. She informs me that she is a medical assistant and has basic life-support training. She is earnest and determined. If there is a heartbeat to bring back to life, she will make sure it happens. We get to thirty compressions, and she offers to take over. I sit back and let her.

"*Thirteen, fourteen, fifteen*," she is counting out loud, and I recheck for a nonexistent pulse. This was death upon impact—I have no doubt in my mind.

The 911 operator instructs us to give rescue breaths. I look at the ashen face and think, between the blood, the asphalt, and my hair color, this stench will now always be a part of my sensate memory. I'll never be able to smell blood like that again without smelling asphalt. I will never be able to smell hair dye leaving the tube without smelling the blood.

"No, no breaths," I tell the woman across from me. I had cooperated with compressions with a sinking nausea, knowing that there was no bringing this woman back to life. But breaths? No breaths.

"She has no pulse," I say out loud to the phone. "She has blood coming from her mouth," I emphasize. "No pulse," I repeat.

The voice on the phone pauses and then relents. "Okay," she agrees, no breaths.

We hear the ambulance sirens approach and within seconds we are surrounded by paramedics, firefighters, and a stretcher.

"I'm a doctor. I've been here for several minutes," I tell the approaching men.

My face, neck, and shoulders are now covered in purple and pink dye, while my hands and arms are stained with dirt and flecks of blood.

"Fixed pupils, no pulse, she was dead when I got here," I say firmly. I have been around enough bodies, alive, and fewer bodies, dead, to know the energetic truth. I had done chest compressions on this woman's shell. Her essence was gone before I arrived.

The paramedics acknowledge that there is nothing more to do. A quick hookup to the heart monitor confirms absent electrical activity. And yet they still do a look around, make eye contact with the two of us huddled around the body.

"We all agree there is nothing more to do?" One of the men glances at each of us, as if we could change this fate. But we nod and a yellow sheet is unfolded.

I am not sure what I expect to feel in the moment, but I do find myself still collapsed on my knees. The medical assistant kneels next to me. The sheet is drawn, and we place hands on the dead woman's legs. One hand on her, one arm around each other. I bow my head while the assistant recites a prayer. The words do not matter. The actual prayer is just a hum in my ignorant ears. But the sentiment, the stranger circle we form to bless and offer peace . . . that I can understand. In that moment, the body under the sheet could be anybody.

The palm of my hand rests on this body's thigh. *Mehry?* My fingers dig in a little bit; the woman to my left squeezes my shoulder. *Where did you go?*

Footsteps behind our group break us out of our vigil and my head pops up, my hand releases.

"You're the doctor? Right?" The police chief approaches.

I give a nod and a shrug as if to say, "Yup, that's me. Yup, a lot of good that did. Yup, the hair thing. Yup. Yup. Yup."

"Thanks for the help. No questions for you. You can go."

I drive home in the slow lane, barely reaching the speed limit. The evening light glows with a neon tint, and I put on sunglasses. The brightness is a contradiction, the sun an insult to the covered body one mile back. Shouldn't the world go dark for just a moment? Shouldn't we all pause?

My hands on the steering wheel are surface-level clean from the antibacterial soap I pumped onto my palms before I left the scene, but the rest of me is covered in remnants of the accident. I know I will strip all my clothes off on the back porch before entering the house. These are clothes I will drop directly into the trash. It won't be the first time.

I dial Alycia on speakerphone. I need to talk to the last person who saw me leave the office, mermaid-hair dream in full effect.

"You're not going to believe what happened," I yell-speak to the empty car.

I describe the traffic slowdown, the body on the road, my first-responder dilemma, the pink dye staining my shirt. She gives me the sympathetic gasps I need in between sad and nervous giggles. I hang up the phone and the car is silent again.

On normal days, I bask in the silence of my car. Right now, though, I am just lonely, and the loneliness invites in all the memories. I am four years old with a foreign name and nobody invites me to their birthday. I am in seventh grade eating lunch with the librarians. I am waking at two in the morning, sneaking out of the house, quietly starting my car, driving on an empty road to the hospital. I am pumping milk in a corner room, staring at a picture of my newborn. I am surrounded by loved ones, family members, lifelong friends, and my mind is not in the room. My body is the empty shell of the woman. *The woman back on the pavement was empty when I arrived.* My face has a fixed look. *Her last expression was already gone.* My smile these days is the upturned pencil line drawn by my daughter when she sits down to color.

I stop at traffic light after traffic light on the seven-mile road home, where apartment buildings become bungalows and trees start to appear next to sidewalks. Numbness is ninety percent of my body, and I try to remember when numb became my new normal. There was a time, I know, when an experience like this one—the encounter with sudden death, the all eyes on me, the futility of my efforts—would leave me shaking and sobbing, overwhelmed with emotion, puffy-faced, and dripping. Nowadays, I clench my back teeth and breathe through my nose when sadness arises. Even now, in the private confines of my car, nobody to see, no person to judge, I cannot summon tears. I stare straight ahead, pay closer-than-usual attention to pedestrians and traffic lights, and feel only the slightest tremble in my body.

The car is too quiet, and I am still ten minutes from home, so I dial my brother, then my best friend, and, finally, my husband. I brief them quickly. I absorb their sympathy. I alter the story of the motorcycle accident each time. My hair gets more color. The children on the road multiply. The stench amplifies. But the facts remain the same. The body is unmoving when I approach. The ribs crack under my compressions. The blood from the lips turns darker with each minute.

It is days later when I learn that the woman on the road was sixty years old. She was a mother, a gardener, and a flower enthusiast. She had wanderlust. She was also a grandmother. *Mehry?* She held her grandbabies close. Knowing these details made me think she might have been amused by the story of the minutes after she died. She might have enjoyed knowing that the person who arrived at the scene of her death was also restless, full of wanderlust, and beauty-seeking. She might have appreciated that ninety minutes after she collided with an old sedan turning into a driveway, the doctor who stared into her unmoving pupils stepped into a shower and watched a brownish stream of water stain the tub. Towel-dried then blow-dried, the purple and aqua, pink and sea-green blended together to form a wave of psychedelic strands. She might have been happy to know: the mermaid hair—it turned out gorgeous.

Grandmother

2018

The hair grew out. Some of the color faded to blond, and over the next six months, trimming the ends left just bits of aqua at the tips. I matched my dress and nails to the color for a family wedding and found myself at a table with my cousins.

"Tell me again about my grandmother." I speak to Navid seated next to me. Her hair falls in one dark, thick sheet down her back. We met each other as kids when she was moving from Iran to the United States and that same hair fell past her waist and almost touched the backs of her knees.

"Our grandmothers were sisters," Navid says. She does what she has done for me a dozen times before—pulls out a paper dessert napkin and uses a ballpoint pen and the squares and circles of Mendelian genetics to draw our family tree. At the top, two circles side by side—her grandmother and mine—sisters.

"That makes us second cousins, once removed," she says, linking several more rows of circles and squares.

"So, basically, sisters too," I reassure us, and put my arm around her shoulders.

She is the closest thing I will have to a sister and our connection runs deep—for decades we have crossed the country to surprise each other with visits, and in 2008 we birthed our oldest boys exactly two months apart, to the day, hour, and minute. One afternoon she accidentally fed my son her breast milk and we felt we had christened our matrilineal bond to the next generation. That night at the wedding, we didn't know that within a year, Navid would be diagnosed with stage four ovarian cancer and find herself shaving her head in the shower to rid herself of the tangled post-chemotherapy dreadlocks.

("I didn't think *I* would lose my hair," she would half laugh, half cry over the phone to me after it happened. "Isn't that ridiculous? Thinking *my* hair would somehow be spared.")

The chairs around us empty as our family members transition from dessert to the dance floor. It's just me and Navid leaning in toward each other.

"What do you know about her?" I turn my attention back to the napkin, fold it, and tuck it into my purse.

"Very little," she answers. "She was so young when she died, you know, and all I've heard is that everybody was so sad."

My mother was the only other person to speak to me about my grandmother.

"My angel always protects me," my mother repeated time and time again.

Once, when my brothers and I were young and she was sick and admitted to the hospital for unknown reasons, my mother reassured us by saying, “My angel is watching over me, don’t worry.”

Later, she described feeling tugged toward the ethereal image of her mother above, floating near the hospital lights. Her body released from her mind and she remembered wanting so badly to join her overhead.

“It’s too soon,” her mother said to her firmly. “Your children still need you. You have to go home to them now.”

I was relieved back then to know the angel looking out for my mom was a reasonable spirit, looking out for us as well.

I turn back to Navid. “I see her around,” I whisper, and she raises her eyebrows.

I don’t mention that one day I was going about my life, and the next, it seemed, my grandmother was there. She crept into my thoughts uninvited—while on walks I felt her drawing me in to rose petals, sending me her scent, asking me to listen. When I was at work, in between patient visits, her voice entered my thoughts unexpectedly. I caught myself talking to her in the passenger seat as I drove home. In my quietest moments, the unmarked minutes between tasks, the gray space of life when we are alone with ourselves, it was like she had never left.

“I think she has something to tell me,” I confess. “I know it sounds strange, but she has something she needs me to know.”

Navid takes a sip of the tea that has appeared in front of her. “I believe it,” she says. “These Iranian grandmothers are very stubborn! They might not leave us alone.”

I laugh. The other day I had picked up my book of poems by the ancient Persian poet Hafiz. Like my ancestors before me, I asked the book a question, flipped open to a random page, and used the words of the poem as an answer.

"Hafiz is a divine envoy," it read, "whom the Beloved has written a holy message upon. . . . Now is the time for the world to know that every thought and action is sacred. . . . Now is the season to know that everything you do is sacred."

Meeting Amelia

2017

For nearly seven years, my days at work are almost always the same—running twenty minutes behind with a waiting room that is starting to fill. This is a typical day in a typical month in my ob-gyn career. I take pride in running the clinic efficiently, but not at the expense of attention and compassion. Often, I *allow* myself to run about twenty minutes behind—any longer and patients begin to rustle around, check in with the front desk, consider complaining, contemplate leaving. Their young children go from mildly content to playing with the blocks or books set out for them to exuberant explorers, opening drawers and uncovering the dark world of speculums, alcohol swabs, Pap smear sticks. My exam rooms transform from the neat-and-tidy spaces for consultations to scenes from a medical carnival, purple exam gloves blown up like balloons, uterus models interacting with toy dinosaurs.

Staying within the twenty minutes or less of running behind maintains order but allows me appropriate license to sit down and actually talk to my patients during their appointments. I can set my laptop to the side. I can breathe while my patient scrolls through her phone's photo library to pull out the latest picture of the baby I delivered. I might drag my chair over, climb onto the counter, grab a tissue box from the top shelf of the supply cabinet, open the perforated cover, and pull out a thin sheet—one for her, one possibly for myself. In the sanctity of my exam room, her assigned patient-chair facing my doctor-stool, with us eye to eye, my chin in my hands, my elbows taking a break on the counter between us, my patient will reveal to me her latest drama. Her boyfriend cheated on her. Her husband passed away. Her dog died. She lost her child to the courts. The herpes test is positive.

My medical assistant walks the short hallway into the waiting room to call for my next patient. I take this moment to click on my schedule for the rest of the afternoon. I need to make sure I do not fall further behind. Everything is on the computer now and my laptop acts as an extension of my left arm. It is a hot mid-July day, I have been working at multiple hospitals, and it has been nearly a year since I have taken a week off. The office air is cool, and I am wearing my uniform of blue hospital scrubs overlaid with my mid-length white coat. My turquoise stethoscope dangles around my neck, my hair is pulled up and away from my face. I apply lipstick in the morning, and again at lunch, but it is faded by now, and most likely my lips carry only the faint undertones of pink lip liner. I feel a weight in the right pocket of my white coat, which houses a small Doppler machine, used for listening to fetal heart tones.

My left pocket holds my phone, quick access for an emergency. Around my neck, tucked under my shirt, is my hospital ID badge, worn in case I get called to the hospital quickly. It bumps against the coolness of my silver Tiffany necklace with my children's initials, the one I wear at heart level every day, the charms gifted to me by my mother at the birth of each one.

My eyes scan the list on my screen. Name, age, condition. Follow-up visit. Repeat Pap smear. New OB visit. I know the first two patients well; we will catch up quickly. The first one will tell me about her mechanic shop and the ways her husband is driving her to insanity. The next will regale me with stories about her online dating misadventures. I will caution her about unprotected sex and her continued risk for an STI. It is what landed her in my office in the first place. She will laugh and say, "I know." And I will leave it at that.

The last patient is new to me. My screen lists "new pregnancy visit" as the reason for the appointment. I click my mouse and quickly glance through this new patient chart, selecting the link to recent chart notes from the primary care doctor who referred her to me. I have about thirty seconds to orient myself. I quickly reread the information—name, age, condition. Name, age, condition. I read over the words again and then one more time, confused and searching for an explanation.

In just that moment, as if we landed on the same line at the same time, my assistant steps away from her desk and begins walking toward me. I look up as I hear her shoes click and I can tell from her short, quick steps, the tightness of her lips, the height of her eyebrows, that she has just seen what I've seen.

My new pregnant patient just checked in. I first read her name and then her age.

"Did you see, Dr. Mary?" She looks at me, her blue eyes blinking fast.

I look up at her, and before I can nod my yes, she blurts, "Your new pregnant patient who just got here? Did you see her age?"

I nod again. Take a breath. For once, I have nothing to say.

Minutes later, I walk into the exam room after a brief pause behind the closed door. I had taken a breath, given a quick knock, turned the door handle, and I was in.

"Hi, I'm Dr. Mary." I glance quickly at the older of the two people in the room. A young girl sits on the exam table, and in the visitor's chair is her mother? Her sister? Their ages confuse me because they both look so young. I internally check my face to make sure my expression remains neutral but friendly, my smile warm but without judgment. I try to perfect my tone—relaxed, nonthreatening.

The older woman digs into her bag and indicates that they have an ultrasound report, and that they saw a doctor yesterday who sent them to me. As she talks, I turn my attention to the exam table and reach out my hand.

"Hi." I grasp the tiny hand of the girl in front of me. "I'm Dr. Mary. What do you like to be called?"

Amelia sits slumped on the edge of the exam table. Although she is at my head level, I have not yet gotten a glimpse of her face. Her back is rounded, one hand outstretched and limply held in my tight grasp. Long, blond hair hangs all around her, down her back, her sides, covering her face. She is petite, barely a hundred pounds, and if she is pregnant, it is not yet obvious to me, her belly well hidden underneath an oversized SpongeBob sweatshirt.

"I'm her aunt," the woman with her says. "She lives with me.

"She's shy," her aunt reports. "And nervous. I told her she was going to have to talk to you, but she's nervous." The woman laughs and I recognize the strain in her voice. They are both terrified. I pause for a moment, looking at the aunt. She has the look of a woman without time for herself, no attempt to brush her hair or apply makeup. Her voice is high-pitched and harsh, with the tremble of a person who has had to defend herself forever.

"Amelia, heeey, Ameeeeliia," I say in a quiet, playful way. I attempt a move that I have never done in my office, a move reserved for children during hurt or sulky moments. I crouch well below the level of her hung head and crane my neck to look up at her, face-to-face. I am practically sitting on the ground, her hair a tent that envelops us both for a moment, and I catch her face with mine.

"Hi!" I say, smiling, with a giggle.

The move works. Nobody wants to see their doctor in such a compromised position, and Amelia sits up quickly, pushing her thick hair away from her eyes, a piece getting caught between her lips, which she spits out.

"There you are!" I say.

She unfolds her body and finally I can see what I am in the room to see: a small bump beneath the sweatshirt. A young girl's face staring at me. No smile on the thin, sad line of her lips. She has the hint of cheekbones that predict her future beauty. Her clear skin is pale in the moment, and she keeps her head steady and still as she begins to take me in. I am surprised by my response to her face. It is not just that it is young, or pretty, but it is sad. Mournfully sad. Gravely and darkly sad. The sadness is gray around her eyes and pink at her neckline. *Sadsadsadsad.* The letters float into my own breath, and I inhale them. Morse code sadness telegraphed in blinks. Braille sadness in the bumps of her skin. I don't know all the languages, but I try. I read the sadness because I believe that is what she needs. And I believe this because from the moment she lifts her head in response to my juvenile peekaboo, she does not look away. Her gaze swallows my face and I am bound in the spell of her very large green eyes. Pleading eyes? Begging eyes? Dead eyes? My body remains calm in the moment, but my thoughts are capital letters pinballing my brain.

"So, I understand that you are pregnant," I begin. I speak directly to Amelia. I know that her aunt is about to chime in. I am already certain that other people have a version of this story to tell. But Amelia has not looked away yet. And because she does not waver, I cannot either.

"Is that right?" I prompt.

I have never engaged in a staring contest like this one—not for fun, and certainly not at work. Amelia sits before me, now straightened and breathing a little faster. It is the only reaction she has given me so far. I can see her chest rise underneath the worn gray of her sweatshirt, SpongeBob arms rising and falling, and I marvel at the stillness of the rest of her body. Has she blinked? Her eyes remain focused, unmoving, boring deep into my head, and as I watch her breathing quicken in response to my question, I try to slow my own breath down.

"The doctor says she is almost six months pregnant," her aunt says, interrupting our silent stance. "She told me she missed her period, so I took her to the doctor and that's what they said."

This much is clear. I confirm the story an hour later, when they finally leave my office, and I call the other clinic.

"It was not that hard to tell that she is pregnant," a nurse says over the phone. "I mean, we just lifted up her shirt and there was the belly."

I had eventually done the same thing in my exam room. I finally asked Amelia to lie back on the table for me, to allow me to touch her belly, measure her uterus with a tape measure, and find the baby's heartbeat with my small Doppler machine.

"Can you feel the baby move?" I speak to her cautiously as I place a pillow under her head, straighten her legs out with a hand underneath her knees. Her sweatshirt is pulled up now, and it is clear that she has been pregnant for a while. The bony limbs of the fetus are almost apparent under her taut abdomen. It is obvious that when the baby moves, her stretched skin rolls and undulates with every kick and turn. Amelia nods silently in response to my question, an almost smile touching the corner of one lip, and her eyes, for the first time, turn on dimly, as if the notion of a baby within is magic enough to bring a sprig of life into her body.

"It does seem like you are about twenty weeks pregnant," I say, my tape measure spanning the bump from her pubic bone to the top of her uterus, measuring exactly twenty centimeters. I chat as I measure, relaxing a little into my role as educator and clinician now that I'm performing some usual tasks. "We can estimate about how far along a pregnancy is by this simple measurement. Not totally accurate, but a quick way to get an idea until we get an official ultrasound," I say, and turn my head to her aunt. We have not spoken yet about the bigger details surrounding the pregnancy, such as what their plans are, whether they have decided to keep the baby, whether other options, including termination or adoption, are available to them. I care about the details of how many weeks a pregnancy is because decisions, such as abortion, depend on that tricky combination of factors that includes religion, politics, superstition, fear, love, and exactly how many weeks since conception.

"The ultrasound you have there was a quick look at the baby," I explain, referring to the pictures they have brought in from a pregnancy resource center. "I would like to get you in for an official ultrasound to look at the baby's anatomy closely and to find out exactly how far along you are." I am speaking to Amelia again but also turn my head toward her aunt.

"We already know it's a boy," her aunt says, clapping her hands and rocking her body. "I'm going to have a nephew!" she squeals with excitement.

It is my turn to freeze. I feel my own breath quicken. Between Amelia, her aunt, the secrecy of the pregnancy until now, and this new, gleeful exuberance, I cannot gauge what is happening in this room.

I've been cautious, gracious to this point, but it is time to address the obvious.

"So, we should talk about Amelia's age." I speak firmly now.

I turn to look back at Amelia. It is only her feelings that I care about in this moment. She is sitting up again, and once again, she is frozen. Her head found its spot, paralyzed atop her neck, and her eyes, those damn green eyes, once again lock onto mine as I speak.

This is when I could lose them, I think, as I keep my own two feet planted, my upper body relaxed. *No false moves*, I tell myself. I am in this with Amelia now. As her aunt speaks, I take in both of them—Amelia's motionless body and penetrating stare, her aunt's aggressive tone.

"From everything we know right now, Amelia had barely started her periods when she became pregnant."

I pause to take in my own words.

The walls of the exam room are painted sky blue. The clinic made the recent decision to cover over the bright yellow walls from the 1980s to create a more calming aesthetic—earthy tones for the waiting room, modern greens and browns for our workstations. Sky blue for the exam rooms, since it is the place where women take off their clothes and spread their legs open for strangers. I enter their bodies, and even their bedrooms, through our conversations. We discuss intimate encounters with lovers, husbands, strangers, best friends.

I am surrounded by sky blue when I look at Amelia and ask her directly, "So, who is the father of this baby?"

Amelia's aunt is quiet for a moment. Amelia has still not spoken a word. The fetal monitor dangles off the counter. I sit on the rolling stool at the foot of the bed where Amelia is seated. My feet grab on to the edge of the bed and allow me to roll closer to her legs. We touch now. I am as close as I can get without crawling onto the bed with her. She continues to watch me, and she stares as I roll into her legs and place a hand on each knee. She looks down; I look up. Her aunt looks at both of us.

I am trying to shrink this big moment into a little moment—like the way I might ask an older patient, "Hey, so who's the father of this baby?" Like, "Soooo, who's the faaaather?" as my program director asked with a smile when I, to my surprise, became pregnant after a few months of dating my future husband in my first year of ob-gyn training.

I do not expect the tears to come as quickly or as intensely as they do. One moment Amelia and I are seated, staring at each other in silence. The next, teardrops are sliding down her cheeks. First quiet and then more rapid, with sobs. Somehow, Amelia maintains her eye contact with me through the blurred distortion of her tears.

Whoa, I think. *Here it comes.* I am certain by her unblinking gaze that she is about to open up to me. That despite her aunt's tense vigil to my left, the invisible bullets of "keep quiet" she shoots, Amelia will tell me. Patients always confess to me in this room. What happened. Who did it. I know she will share how, in this goddamn world of mothers and aunties and grandmothers, a near-child gets spread, penetrated, impregnated, and arrives on my exam table twenty or so weeks later.

"Hey." I say this quietly, just between me and her. "It's okay. Take your time."

Keeping one hand on her leg, I roll slightly to grab a box of tissues off the counter, place it on my lap, and hand her several at a time.

Her aunt chimes in. Interrupts the tears.

"She always cries when we talk about this." Her voice is shrill and unyielding, no room for empathy-silence or Kleenex.

I resist the urge to shoot her a dark look. I want her out of the room, but I haven't summoned the courage to ask her to leave.

I am feeling a little terrified. In our short time together, this woman and I have sized each other up. An eager-to-please doctor faced with an I-don't-give-a-shit-about-you aunt. In any battle—of wits, mind, or strength—I am pretty sure she would win.

It is a painful few minutes. Ten? Fifteen? Amelia is sobbing, her hands covering her face, blowing her nose into the wad of tissues.

Her hair is matting around her cheeks, and she wipes at strands sticking to her lips.

I try hard during the crying to keep still. No gestures. I feel the numbing effect of my bent legs start to travel into my feet. But with Amelia's tears, just the sheer amount of liquid pooling out of her unflinching eyes, the growing dark spots on her sweatshirt, her jeans, it feels imperative not to move. My hands have remained rested on her knees, and occasionally a warm tear lands on the top of my hand. Is that okay? she asks in her look, and I use one breath to nod with my eyeballs. What is this conversation we are having, her eyes to mine?

Finally, with a slowing of sniffles, Amelia's mouth begins to form words. I see her lips initiate a tiny motion and I try not to lean forward.

"I don't know how this happened," she whispers. Her head shakes and the words come spilling out. "I can't remember, I can't remember, I can't remember." She shakes. "I don't know how this happened."

In my years of undergraduate premedical studies, four years of medical school training, and then four more years of ob-gyn residency, I learned, in detail, the molecular structure of carbon, the devious workings of a virus, and the pathophysiology of antibiotic resistance. I dissected tissue from dozens of tiny nerves that lead from the bicep muscle into the hand. I memorized EKG tracings, interpreting blips of lines and spaces as keys to life. I pulled thirty-six-hour shifts with no sleep and zombielike encounters in the emergency room, perking up for emergency C-sections and ruptured tubal pregnancies at two in the morning. I studied for exams so many hours in a row that I developed actual boils on the backs of my thighs and chewed my fingernails to nubs every couple of weeks. I delivered twin babies with joyous tears and held in my arms the sobbing patient whose baby was delivered without a heartbeat. Patients nearly bled to death upon entering the emergency room with miscarriages, and I sped to the hospital, ignoring red lights and traffic rules. Even when my heart was pounding so fast and hard, I have held a frozen calm smile and reassured patients, their husbands, their parents, and their friends that everything was going to be okay. Thousands of hours of training to deal with nearly any emergent or unexpected situation. And yet, in this second, in the minutes after Amelia erupted with those words, "I can't remember," I find myself totally unprepared.

"I don't know how this happened." Amelia's round doe eyes have not left my face. But now they are wide and panicked, her face reddened by all the crying.

"You don't remember?" I push myself back from her knees, sit straight up, and feel myself shutting down. The caution and care I have tried to sustain become overwhelmed by something in me that feels like rage. "You don't know how this happened?!" I am breathing faster and still trying to maintain composure, but everything in this room feels wrong. The pregnant child. The defensive relative. The light-blue walls. My starched white coat and its imposter air of competence and authority.

"She doesn't want to tell us and get in trouble." Amelia's aunt is standing now, gathering her bag and effectively ending the conversation. "We have to go."

I look at her aunt, who looks at Amelia, who is looking at me. Am I supposed to let her go now? Can I actually allow her to leave the room, go back to whatever unknown place she came from?

"I feel very uncomfortable letting you leave like this," I say, more to the aunt than to Amelia. I hate that my voice sounds apologetic, almost meek.

"Well, we're going." The aunt motions to Amelia, and Amelia slowly rises to her feet, shuffling toward the door. Her shoulders slump again, her hair is a shield once more, and her eyes are returned to their downward gaze. The moment between us has passed and my opportunity yields to the aunt.

Don't let her walk out of this office! the voice inside me screams. "I will call you tomorrow after the ultrasound" is what comes out instead.

"I want to see you back here next week, Amelia," I call out to her. They are already out the door, walking into the waiting room and toward the exit. "Every week," I call out again.

They do not look backward. She shuffles and slumps, and her aunt gives her back a little shove out of the office. I watch through a frosted window between the waiting room and clinic space, not sure whether I will see her again.

After Amelia and her aunt leave, I sit at the desk in my office and stare at the computer screen. I have to document my visit with Amelia. And I have to call the Department of Human Services (DHS). I am a mandatory reporter for suspected child abuse. I reach for the phone, my hand bumping into the photo of my family sitting on the desk. Keith and I, our son at the age of three, and our baby girl. She is plump-cheeked in the photo, not yet stretched long and lean, her hair still coming in wispy. She sits on my lap with my grinning son on one side and my husband on the other. We are smashed together as close as possible. Smiles. Arms wrapped and mixed up in each other. I think about how badly I wanted to become a mother. When Keith came along, there was no forethought or planning; it just happened. Our babies entered, precious, into our lives. We might have felt whole before they were born, but we exploded with wonder after they arrived. I look at my daughter's cherub face, so innocent, so plump with possibility, and tap my finger to the picture as if to touch her face.

I bring my finger to my lips, give it a kiss, and pick up the phone. I cannot fathom a scenario in which a preteen girl becomes pregnant, then claims she cannot remember how it happened, and that girl is not a victim of abuse.

"I am calling to report my suspicion of child abuse, sexual abuse. I am a physician," I say after someone answers the phone.

The phone call with DHS is brief and unsatisfying. Yes, they are aware of this case. Yes, yes, yes. Thank you for the call. Yes, there is also a detective assigned to the case who will be going to the house.

Yes. Yes. Thank you.

I shut down my computer and walk through the office, turning off lights. I am the last one in the building, and I am ready to go home.

"Hey, I'm on my way." It is my routine phone call as I start the engine and back out of the parking space.

"Heeeey! All right! Awesome!" I hear the buzz of our children in the background, music playing. "Dinner's almost ready. Come on home!"

Pulling into my driveway, I blink, surprised that I am already there. I can't even remember the drive, having changed lanes and stopped at lights on autopilot. I know what is about to greet me: the bright faces of my kids. The two of them competing at the door to open it first, to run onto the porch. It is a mother's dream: bursting, happy children; a husband keeping the house together, cooking dinner, guiding the setting of the table and picking up of toys. My job is to go to work and return in one piece, to try to remain as grounded as possible. To allow my day at the office to evaporate before I click open my car door and step outside. To transform from doctor to mama.

"Mama! Mama!" The kids are at my legs, my daughter fighting her brother to be held. I bend over and pick her up. Her bird bones render her light as a balloon. She nuzzles her face into my neck and I plant kisses all over her exposed cheek. My son is calmer, more refined. He leans his head into my hip and I scratch the top of his head.

"How are you guys? How was your day?!" I force brightness into my voice. An uplift, a higher pitch. My family deserves sunshine. From under a dark cloud, I strain to bring out the shiniest smile I can imagine.

I set my daughter down and immediately she is calling for me.

"Mama! Come!" She tugs on my pant leg and my son peeks from behind the kitchen door. "Come play with us!"

"I'm coming, I'm coming." I try to keep my voice steady again. "Just let me get changed."

I walk into the bedroom and close the door behind me. I just need a minute. I need a minute. Changing into pajama bottoms and a sweatshirt, I stare at my bed and pause. Don't crawl under the covers, I implore myself. You can't crawl under the covers.

"Mama!" Their voices are at the door and my time is up. I have been gone for a couple of days due to work. Two days we have gone without breakfast together or bedtime kisses. As much as I need to disappear, to hide from the reality of Amelia and the saga I had entered, I need to walk out of my bedroom door more.

"Mama, come out!" My daughter's voice is insistent on the other side of the bedroom door.

I can hear my son behind her. "She's coming, she's coming," he says, always the diplomat.

I open the door and walk into the rest of our night. Obstacle courses in the basement. Tickle fights. Dinner on the back deck, listening to the wind breeze in and blow away. Bubble baths. Bedtime stories. Snuggles under the covers in between the two of them. My daughter's damp hair on my chest. My son's heavy breathing onto my cheek. All of us with drooping eyelids and slowed heartbeats. Keith tiptoeing upstairs, covering us with a blanket, and turning off the light.

Twenty Weeks

2017

The next morning, I am sitting on the Labor and Delivery floor of my hospital. I have patients in labor, and I am in front of a computer monitor that scrolls heart rates and contraction patterns. Babies' heart rates bump and rise across the screen, and I am reassured by the electronic lines of the fetal monitor, lines I read like song lyrics: *I'm okay, beat beat, you're okay, beat beat, we're okay, beat beat beat.*

The hospital feels quiet. Nurses check in and dispense medication. An occasional newborn cries out from behind closed postpartum doors. Sleepy fathers wander into the kitchen for coffee. I perch in front of the screens, prepare to make a phone call, dial the number, and wait.

Today I sent Amelia for a formal ultrasound, and she should be back at home now. Measuring her baby accurately and assessing how far along she is in her pregnancy is my first pressing need, even above deciphering her social situation, above understanding her family dynamic, above unraveling the secret of the pregnancy. My job, as her doctor, is to provide her with options. To figure out what those options are and explain them like items on a menu—turn the biggest decision in life into a palatable list, complete with pros and cons: (1) Keep baby. Pros. Cons. (2) Consider adoption. Pros. Cons. And on and on.

It is a strange role to be placed in between a girl who is pregnant and her legal guardians. The laws in our country blur when it comes to pregnancy. On the one hand, with pregnancy comes emancipation—the ability to make legal decisions in most states. To accept procedures without consent from an adult. In some states pregnancy enables them to request and receive an abortion. On the other hand, every other facet of the child's life is at the mercy of their adult. Amelia does not have money. She cannot drive. For her to remain in the home of the adults caring for her, to remain in "good graces," her decisions must align with theirs. Otherwise, where to go?

I feel the weight of this within me as I listen to the phone ring. Normally, I call my patients directly. However, with Amelia as young as she is, it does not feel appropriate. With permission from Amelia, I will also talk to her aunt about the ultrasound. I imagine them both pressed to the phone, listening on speaker.

"The baby is measuring twenty weeks and two days. This is an important number," I hear myself say.

In the pediatric medical world, twenty-two weeks is generally a very early cutoff used to predict "fetal viability." This means that if a baby is born after twenty-two weeks, there is a chance for survival. A full-term pregnancy is forty weeks, an extra five months of developing naturally within the mother's uterus. Although extremely premature, babies born after only twenty-two weeks may have a chance at survival, depending on multiple factors. Doctors might perform full resuscitations. Weak, translucent, Coke can–sized fetuses will endure extreme measures to keep them alive. Incubators serve as surrogate wombs. Advanced technology supports their tiny lungs and hearts in order to promote growth and maturity. Incredible efforts will keep them warm, assess their brains, and promote contact with their mother and father. Holidays will come and go. Pumpkin hats and Santa socks will decorate their skeletal bodies.

Some will not survive. Devastated parents, nurses, and doctors will weep and bury infants in doll-sized coffins. Some will undergo surgeries, have deficiencies, and face challenges throughout their lives. Some will defy all expectation. They will grow and go home and eventually walk back onto the pediatric floor of the hospital that saved their life. They will bring cakes and flowers on their birthdays and discuss hitting all the usual milestones. They will graduate from college. Twenty-two weeks. It is a critical milestone.

Amelia's baby is under twenty-two weeks. State by state, decisions are made regarding abortion and legal limits. Where we live, being under twenty-two weeks means Amelia might still have time to choose termination.

"This decision, this path, this choice, is not mine to make." Those words tumble out of my mouth. "I just need your family to know all the options."

I can tell her aunt is listening closely. She answered the phone on the first ring and shushed the other children in the background.

Now there is breath between us. And silence. Again, as I did for Amelia in the office, I hold the silence and feel my sweat. There is so much noise in our silence.

"Here are the places you can go, should you choose to terminate at this stage. Let me know if you have any questions."

She replies with a thank-you. We click off, easing our discomfort.

I am alone again, with the labor computer monitor ticking away. I turn to the reassurance of the screen. Another patient's baby rhythmically marking time until entry into the world. A baby with parents of a different generation. Older. Married. Ready. Excited. I watch the heartbeat tracing and imagine the pea-sized heart of Amelia's baby. Yesterday, we smiled and cooed at its *clip-clop* sound over the speaker held to her swollen belly. A heartbeat that could tell a story. We shared a human minute, Amelia and I and her aunt. As daughters and mothers. As breathing animals with hearts of our own.

I feel my body sink against the chair and my head falls back. Dammit. I close my eyes. Clench my fists. Breathe. How do we ask women to make choices about their pregnancies when the pregnancy itself was clearly not a choice?

"Doctor," I hear, and feel a tap on my shoulder. It's a labor nurse. "She's ready. Your patient in the room. She says she feels the urge to push."

It's nice to have a distraction from Amelia, and I walk down the hallway to meet my laboring patient. In the world of labor and deliveries, we sometimes enter a room not knowing what might greet us on the other side—an eager professional couple finally having their baby after years of infertility, or a newly immigrated family celebrating with flowers and food, or the all-alone single mother hoarding syringes of heroin in her purse, later to be discovered on the floor of the bathroom.

In this moment, I approach a door and hear something new, not the usual groans of labor but, instead, a woman's voice singing a church hymn—loud, crisp, angelic. I enter and see a woman sitting upright in bed, dark hair in twisted pigtails, red lipstick on her lips and dotted on rounded cheeks. She has sweat across her forehead, and with each labor contraction she raises her face to the ceiling, closes her eyes, and uses her voice to ask for guidance.

"*Oh God, hold my hand,*" she sings with a voice that cuts through the beeps of her blood pressure cuff and summons a strength possibly larger than herself. "*Help me through this pain.*" Her voice is clear with vibrato and melody. Her body rocks and she places her hands around her tight belly.

The nurse and I look at each other, and then back at our patient. I am mesmerized by her voice, the kind of gospel that forces goose bumps and inadvertently tears up my eyes. More than that, I am touched by her appeal for help. Many patients are numb from an epidural at this point, and they often look to me, seated in between their legs, one eye on the computer monitors, for a cue that they are contracting. Others turn inward or to the person next to them, breathing or wailing in agony. I, myself, often ignored my body's cues for assistance. I frequently pushed past warning signals of fatigue, dehydration, or hunger. This one, though, she knows to ask for help. And she knows how to do it in a most ethereal, gorgeous way.

I stand by her side for a few minutes with my hand on her low back and then position myself at the end of the bed. She is ready to begin pushing, and I use my gloved fingers to guide pressure onto her perineum, gently touch the top of her baby's head. With her head propped on pillows, her dark pigtails splayed, she changes the words to her hymn.

"*Doctor*," she sings, looking directly into my face. "*Tell me what to dooooo.*" I cannot control my smile of delight. I am being summoned by song, my expertise called upon by this siren.

"Deep breath in," I direct, holding her face with my eyes. "And bear down, everything into the pressure."

"*Thank you, Doctorrrrrrrr*," her crooning continues, and she does precisely as instructed, craning her head to face me, then the nurse to her right and the nurse to her left. Her partner is not available to be with us, and so we form her birthing circle. We are the parishioners of her church. After twenty minutes of earnest pushing alternating with hymn, her newborn son joins us, dark-haired, pink, and crying. I place him onto her belly, and she clutches him, tears flowing. She turns her voice from the ceiling to her newborn and welcomes him into the world as if an angel has shepherded him into life.

While waiting for the placenta to deliver, I am able to take a moment to pause for myself. The new mother, baby, and her nurse make welcoming cooing sounds from the bed, and I fold my gloved hands in my lap. Sometimes my job is just to wait patiently for the body to do its natural thing. The oxytocin release from delivering the baby will now signal the placenta to separate, and soon there will be signs that it is also delivering. I have learned to use this time just to wait. My own adrenaline is exiting my cells—no matter the type of birth, there is a crescendo and the subsequent release of energy inside of me as well. When it all goes well, as in this situation, my body can relax from its fight or flight, my muscles release off their bones. I keep an eye on the light bleeding between her legs to make sure nothing picks up, and my thoughts wander back to the phone call with Amelia and her family. I feel my desire to protect her as if she were my own daughter, to scoop her up and swaddle her like the tiny new life in front of me.

I watch the umbilical cord hanging out of the patient start to elongate, a sign that the placenta is ready, and I know that my ability to intervene is limited. Just like now, I play an accessory role, an extra in their story—here to ensure a safe passage and then I'm gone. With barely any traction on the cord, the placenta exits her body and plops into the basin. This birth is complete.

"Thank you, Doctor." The mother's shining eyes and red-lipstick smile lock onto my face. "I will never forget this," she says.

I wash her sticky belly and inner thighs with warm soapy water, then move up to her head to take a close look at the newborn tucked under her arm.

"Thank *you*," I say. I needed this too, I think to myself, this reminder of an everyday miracle. I squeeze a hug around her shoulders, blow a kiss to her baby, and allow her humming lullaby to serenade me out of the room.

A System Broken

2017

I see Amelia once a week for the remainder of her pregnancy. Her aunt asks whether weekly is necessary, and I tell her yes.

After my phone call regarding the ultrasound, her aunt made it clear that they are "going to have the baby." At their next appointment I get up the nerve I need and ask her aunt to leave the room.

It is the first time I am alone with Amelia, and we both need a second to adjust. I walk around the bed with my measuring tape and fetal Doppler. We do the usual things—listen to the heartbeat, talk about the baby's movement. Amelia barely speaks. She answers my questions with one word and keeps her head pointed down.

I do what will become normal for us during these appointments. I sit on my stool and wheel myself in. Again, at her knee level. My face looking up at hers. One of my palms on each of her knees.

"So, did you guys talk about plans for the baby?" I ask in as steady a voice as possible.

"Yes."

"Aaaaaand, what are your thoughts?"

Amelia looks up and, surprised, I push away from her. For the first time since we met, she starts talking.

"They called a clinic. They talked about it. And then my aunt told me that if I had an abortion, that the baby would come back to haunt me. That his soul would be out there, and I would be haunted by the baby forever."

She says the words fast and excitedly and sounds, for the first time, like a normal kid.

"Okay," I answer. My job is not to express any opinion when it comes to theories around abortion and the soul of a fetus.

"And what about adoption?"

"My aunt said that the baby would grow up and find out he was adopted and that he would hate me. And because he hated me, he would haunt me too."

Amelia disappears back into her stare.

"In the end, it is up to you." I say this firmly. "In the end, it is your body and the rest of your life. You get to decide."

Stare.

Stare.

The appointment is over.

I feel like I am in the trenches with Amelia and her family. A deep hole of confusion on my part and secrecy on theirs. Week after week we meet—sometimes with her aunt in the room, sometimes alone. Amelia becomes more comfortable, and I feel like we develop an actual relationship. She occasionally smiles. She greets me now with a story or two about her week. About how hungry she is all the time. About how much the baby moves. We discuss visits by DHS and a state-assigned nurse. She scrunches her nose and rolls her eyes when we talk about these women. She finds them condescending and weird. She says they speak loudly to her as though she can't understand what they are saying. She admits that when they are around, she barely talks.

I grow more at ease in my role as her doctor and advocate. I learn that if I want to turn off Amelia's voice, return her back to the stony state she was in when we first met, all I have to do is hint a question about the father of the baby and she disappears. So, I stick with the medical details, update her on what to expect at each stage of pregnancy. In between appointments, I check back in with DHS, a system that is overworked and under-resourced. The people who answer the phone know my voice and transfer me to the appropriate caseworker, who is often away from her desk.

"What about the detective on the case? What does he say?" I ask someone when I am finally connected to a person.

"You can discuss that with him directly." The woman on the other end is trying to be polite, but she knows nothing she says will satisfy me.

"There are other girls in that family," I say, raising my voice. "I am worried about all of them."

"Look, Doctor. Thank you for your concern. But you do your job, and we will do ours."

Week after week I approach my appointments with Amelia with hope and enthusiasm, determined to make progress with her family, convinced I can help secure a safe environment for her. Each time I return home a deflated-balloon version of myself.

I find out who the detective on the case is and I call him once a week. I give him credit. He has interviewed the entire family, relatives, and acquaintances.

"Nobody is talking," he finally tells me around week four of my phone calls. "This family knows the system. And they know how to work with the system. If nobody talks, nothing can happen—nobody to blame, no ability to remove the children."

"You can't check any other way? No paternity test? No DNA?" My frustration turns my voice shrill.

"Not without permission. We are signing off the case for now."

"Seriously! That's it? With other girls in the house? And Amelia still living there?"

"The reality is we have many cases and many children in situations worse than this—like the ones being locked in a basement and not being fed."

I feel my eyebrows shoot up and my eyes open wide. He is losing his patience with me, and that example feels both terrifyingly real and meant to shut me up.

"We will do what we can, and we have until she turns eighteen to figure it out." He hangs up.

I stare at the disconnected phone in my hand, then throw it onto the chair, where it bounces and drops to the floor. I feel hot tears form. My training has not actually taught me how to deal with this.

Somebody's Babies

2017

When Amelia goes into labor, I am there. When my colleagues in high-risk obstetrics give the green light for her to attempt a vaginal birth, I trust them. Although I worry that the bony structure of her pelvis might not be adequate, that her hips are not wide enough to allow the baby to descend, in the end, I allow the decision for her to proceed.

"She's in labor." I take the phone call partway through a clinic day when Amelia's aunt calls. In this regard, I trust her. She has birthed a few children herself. She knows what labor looks like. I tell her I will meet them at the hospital.

For the afternoon Amelia progresses like most women in labor. She breathes and groans, walks then rests. We place her in a bathtub with warm jets where she closes her eyes in between the painful contractions. I cancel my afternoon and my evening and the rest of my night. Now that we are at the finish line, I plan on staying by her side until this is over.

"Amelia, you are doing great." I stand with a hand on her sacrum as she bends over herself, holding her body up next to the bed. Her aunt stands vigil in one corner, rocking and biting her fingernails. Witnessing her nervousness, I think for a moment that maybe I have read her wrong. Maybe she will show up in the end—for her niece, for the baby, for this family. Maybe, after all I have seen and heard, Amelia will be okay.

Before midnight, Amelia is ready to begin pushing. The epidural has been placed, and she has slept for a few hours. I take advantage of her sleep to finally rest and spend the evening at the nurses' station.

"We don't understand what's going to happen with the baby," the nurses say, buzzing about the family. "Who takes care of the baby?"

"One thing at a time," I am able to say. "First, let's safely deliver him."

When Amelia gets to ten centimeters dilated, even with the epidural she feels the pressure to push. We prepare the room for delivery. I sit on the edge of the bed and coach her on when and how to push.

"You'll take a break in between the contractions," I tell her. "And then, when you feel the pressure build, we will help you pull your legs back and you will bear down." I take a deep breath and do a pretend bearing down, bugging out my eyes and blowing out my cheeks in an exaggerated way to make her laugh and show her what not to do.

She smiles, tired. She has been mostly quiet throughout the labor, especially once she became comfortable with the epidural.

But I know her by now, and I see a little sparkle in her eyes. She is nervous, but she is also excited.

"Okay! Ready to do this?"

She nods.

I gesture toward her aunt to grab a leg. I don't know whether she and I will ever be straight with each other, but in this moment, there is a job to get done, and we will do it as a team.

"Deep breath. Okay and push. And a quick breath in. And push again."

The words come out of me over and over again. *I could say them, with this rhythm, in this tone, in a coma*, I think to myself. She is my athlete. I am her coach. This is our Olympics.

When a patient is just a few pushes away from delivery, the top of the baby's head wiggles and slides just a little bit extra with each push. The pubic bone is being cleared—this is what we call crowning. After an hour and a half of pushing, with sweat beads on Amelia's forehead and her aunt's voice encouraging, we are crowning.

"Just pause for a moment." I look at Amelia with a smile. "Let me get my gown and two gloves on. Then we'll meet your baby."

For a moment the room shifts from the serene metronome of the pushing process to a flurry of activity. The baby warmer is switched on and an additional nurse enters the room. I separate the bottom of the bed and we place Amelia's legs in stirrups. I gown and glove and turn back to her.

"I need to push," she then says, loud now.

With three swift pushes a baby boy is delivered—first the head, then shoulders and body. I do what I always do—offer to place the baby on her belly for immediate skin-to-skin contact—but Amelia looks at the slime-covered, blood-speckled child and asks us to take him away. I clamp the umbilical cord and look at her aunt to see who is going to cut the cord.

"I'll do it." Her aunt steps forward, and with a swift swipe of the scissors, the cord is disconnected, the baby is wrapped in a blanket, and placed on a warmer for the nurses.

Almost immediately, Amelia hemorrhages. In fact, she loses over half of her blood volume in the hour following the delivery. The baby is out. The placenta is out. The uterus is firm and contracting down. And she is bleeding uncontrollably onto my lap.

Hemorrhage is a leading cause of maternal death. But not on my watch. Not in this country with all the drugs to stop bleeding, to make the uterus clamp down, the procedures, the interventional radiology, the option for an emergency hysterectomy. I deal with postpartum hemorrhages all the time, so I go through the motions quickly. First this med, then that one. Make sure she has good IV access. Make that two. Start fluids. Check blood pressure. Get anesthesia into the room. Get an extra nurse. Check blood pressures again. "Amelia? Amelia? You okay?" "She's looking pale." Check a blood count, check a pulse. Order blood. Start transfusing.

All of this is happening, and she continues to bleed. Eventually a table is set up behind me to track the numbers of sutures and lap pads I am using. It is more than we have ever seen. I tick off all the usual suspects: She is not bleeding from the uterus. The entire placenta is out. The cervix is not torn. She is bleeding from her vagina, which essentially has exploded. All I can say is that her barely pubescent vagina has exploded.

While she is bleeding, and I am sewing and putting on pressure and sewing again, trying to catch every bleeding shred of tissue I can grasp, her aunt is pacing and watching me.

"Is she okay, Doctor? What's going on? Is she okay?"

I cannot look up at her. I am focused on tracking the flow of blood. But I answer and explain, then keep answering and explaining for forty-five minutes.

"She is bleeding. A lot. I am just trying to get it under control. But she is stable. Right, Amelia, you doing okay?"

Amelia lets out a quiet "I'm okay."

"We are giving her blood to keep up with what she has lost. How is she?" I redirect to anesthesia.

"She is stable. Her blood pressures are stable. We are about to finish the first unit of blood."

It is a first for me, this tiny, exploded vagina. I sew and cut and place pressure and start again, package after package of suture material opened and thrown on the table behind me.

"We've got this, Amelia, okay?" I speak to her in the same motherly, assuring tone I've always used with her.

And then I look at her aunt, who looks more scared than I have ever seen her. *How fucked-up is this situation?* I think. I am sewing up the vagina of a baby who just had a baby. An almost baby just had a baby.

I finally stop. After thirty-two packages of sutures and sixty lap pads I call for gauze—a thin strip of tape-like material that can be packed into the vagina. I thread it with a pair of forceps and just pack and pack and pack until I cannot fit any more. I place pressure on the remaining oozing vessels and pray that tamponade with the cotton will be enough. I push as much gauze as I can fit into the space, then I sit and watch and wait. The bleeding has slowed down.

"It looks like it's going to be okay," I tell her aunt. "But I'm not moving from here for at least an hour. You should lie down."

“Okay,” she relents. “Hey, Doctor?” She stares me straight in the face before walking toward the side couch, and I catch the quickest flash of relief when she says, “Thank you.”

I nod. And turn back to inspect the packing.

Her aunt and I speak one final time the next afternoon. It is the last time I will ever see her. We all spend the night in the hospital, and by morning, the baby is doing well, Amelia is feeling better, and her aunt is rested and energetic.

“Hey, can I speak with you?” I tap her arm after checking on Amelia.

I need to go home, to take a shower, to take a break. But I feel like I have one last opportunity to get through to the family. DHS has been alerted that the baby was born, and a social worker is involved in the case. By all reports, they will clear Amelia’s family and Amelia will likely go home with the baby tomorrow, as his legal guardian.

“Sure.” Her aunt walks out of the room with me, leaving Amelia asleep in the bed and the baby asleep in a bassinet.

I guide her to the nursery, where we can talk behind the closed door. The aunt is the same height as I am but double my weight. She wears hospital scrubs and today, so do I. I imagine how we look—two tired, unshowered women in a nursery standoff. I share with her my relief that Amelia and the baby are okay, and that the delivery was difficult but everybody was recovering. She nods her head in quiet agreement.

“So, look.” I change my tone. I am going to keep my voice steady and firm. She is not going to intimidate me today. There is now a baby involved.

“There’s a lot of talk about the father of this baby,” I continue.

She stares.

"People are saying things." I keep going and she remains silent.

"People are wondering if you know who the father is." I just have to keep going or I might not say it. "If it's someone who lives at the house."

She shifts her stance. And then suddenly speaks.

"You think I care what other people think and what other people are saying?" Her face comes closer to my face. "If I cared what people said, you think I would be here today?"

Breathe, I tell myself. "DHS is involved now, so it's their job to figure things out."

"That's right," she answers.

"But since you don't know who it is, why not do some paternity tests? You know, try to figure it out?"

Eye to eye and face-to-face. Me holding her stare. Her eyes squinting for just a second at me.

"And I know those tests are expensive, so we can figure that part out, maybe protect Amelia in the future?"

She looks at me. For the first time in our tense relationship, she does not rebut me right away. But it is the look that says she knows my game. She is onto me. I think I am so clever, but we both know I am less clever than she is. She has been winning this one all along.

"I don't need to prove anything to anybody." She turns around and walks out the door.

Supply and Demand

2017

Something happens to me after Amelia delivers her baby. Somewhere in between stopping her hemorrhage and sending her off with implanted birth control at her six-week postpartum visit, I feel myself unravel. She will continue to exist in a world where the truth of her pregnancy would only be shared among a few. Her baby will somehow survive and grow in both the shadow and the light of this truth. And I, the doctor, will also carry on. There will be other patients and mistruths. Some of their pregnancies will also be shrouded in secret and mythology. Their suffering will briefly brush the edges of my life, leave a momentary mark, and then fade.

I begin to work harder than ever. Every moment not working feels like a missed opportunity to improve a life, to do better than I did before. Work as a survival strategy feels integrated into my cells, the invisible inheritance of immigrant kids—an imprinting that began young for me, passed down from my father. When people ask me what it took to become a doctor, what were the sacrifices I made, how hard did I have to work, I tell them that I have been working hard since kindergarten. Those days, my toughest lessons began in the car on the way to school, everything else taught in the classroom simple compared to being in the passenger seat for that fifteen-minute drive.

Even today, I can see the silver-blue Mercedes humming in the driveway, exhaust forming clouds in the crisp morning air. "Go, go, go," my mother said as she handed us each a lunch box and kissed our heads. We scrambled out the door.

"It's your turn," my brother called as he tugged the back seat door open. My gut clenched. I was riding shotgun that day.

"Ready?" My father leaned back into his seat, took the steering wheel, and shifted the car into reverse. His voice was deep and graveled—his morning voice—but penetrating. As we grew older, our friends referred to my father as the largest six-foot man in the world. Whether this illusion of a giant came from the oversized head, the ears that stretched from temple to chin, the amount of dark hair that he combed back from his forehead, or his sheer earthly presence, I still wonder. He was funny, spontaneous, booming at times. Quiet, moody, fist-banging mad in less fortunate moments. For now, Earl Grey steamed from his teacup nestled between us, balanced in the cup holder, hot waves nearly splashing out of an actual glass teacup.

"Let's review where we left off." His deep voice cut through the quiet hum in the car.

"We were talking about supply and demand," he said as he

brought the rim of the glass to his lips, sipped, glanced toward me, then set it down. His eyes were a beautiful light blue. An Iranian with blue eyes? I would get that question as I grew older. Fair skin, light hair, my father with his blue eyes. It's how many Iranians look, I would answer. We come from all over Europe and Asia. Iran for Aryan. Get it? Decades later the question, and the answer, remain the same.

"So, the problem is . . . if a company is producing, for example, lumber, wood to build houses, and a big fire happens and half of the wood burns, what happens to the price of wood? Does it go up or down?"

"Ummm . . ." I spent my back-seat-of-the-car mornings reading about becoming a Russian ballerina. Questions about lumber, fire, and the price of wood felt far from my priorities.

I thought about the last time I was in the jump seat. When I was unable to answer the question correctly. The irritation with me was obvious and I left the car ashamed, with hidden tears.

"Up," my brother whispered to me through the crack between the front and back seats.

"Up?" I said softly. My dad nodded with pride.

There was nothing, truly nothing, my father wanted more for me than to become a doctor. He had overcome great tragedy in his life to end up in medical school in Shiraz, followed by residency at Johns Hopkins, then a fellowship at the University of Illinois. He specialized in infectious disease and took immense pride in his work through the eighties and nineties AIDS epidemic in California, and in his decades of commitment to the poorest, lowest-income communities outside of San Francisco. He treated abscesses caused by heroin poppers and solved medical mysteries that stumped every other specialist. He was considered a legend and a saint, a genius and a savior by his colleagues, his patients, and his friends. There was not a phone call he would not take no matter the time of night, and no challenge he did not meet. He might have been viewed as a larger-than-life giant by others, but he was my personal giant, and I wanted nothing more than to earn his respect and acceptance.

Like all first-generation Americans, I knew early on what immigration meant for my parents: discrimination based on their accents, no matter how perfect their English became, a lost connection to extended family, and that sense of absolutely wanting to belong where they live. There was also the possibility of never returning home, as politics or economics or social structures might not safely allow them back. For my Iranian parents, this was especially true.

Through all my years of childhood, I never heard my parents speak of sacrifice or loss; they spoke only of opportunity. They focused their conversations with us on how fortunate and beautiful it was to raise children in a country where their daughter could grow up to become whatever she wanted, where there was no ceiling to any of our future successes. Ideas about what we would accomplish seemed to overwhelm any thoughts they had about what they missed about Iran. Their hope for us was clear.

In my twenties I spent several years pursuing my personal ambitions—enrolling in a graduate program in communications, training in Shotokan karate, living on a sailboat. During our weekly phone calls, I could feel my father's worry that my future career in medicine was spiraling off course, and one spring, he and my mother invited me to join them on a weeklong vacation in Paris. We stumbled upon the Musée Picasso and spent hours lingering over the sketches and paintings in an exhibit focused on Picasso's early work, years before he produced anything we might recognize. We studied piece after piece, reading each description, both of us equally entranced by the evolution of an artist whose work would come to transform the art world.

"So, I have to ask you," my father said, hours later, as we sat on a bench outside the museum licking ice cream cones. It was the type of day in Paris I might have dreamt about as a girl. The park bench surrounded by grass so green it appeared neon. Young couples lying on picnic blankets with their bodies interlaced, nibbling, giggling. My dad outstretched his arm around my shoulder and turned to look at me. I was twenty-six years old to his fifty-nine. The only difference in his appearance from my childhood days was the graying of his hair. His blue eyes still shone. His giant features barely sagged. It was still the face I loved more than almost any other face I knew.

"When are you going to get serious about your life?" He cleared his throat.

I stared at one of the couples lying underneath the tree in front of us. They were a Monet painting come to life, she in a dress with a wide-brimmed straw hat; he with pink cheeks and a white smile, turned on his side to stare at her face. They were enraptured with each other, and I could not look away.

"I feel like I am serious about my life," I whispered. I could not believe we were having this talk. Again.

"Because, you know . . ." he started. And I knew.

"If you sent in your application for medical school now, you could start next year. . . ."

There was only one path to acceptance. I needed to become a doctor.

"The thing is," he continued. And I wish I'd never heard the line that came next.

"If you had some big talent . . . like Picasso had a talent. He was an artist. Or if you had another talent. Like in music, or something else . . ." His words trailed off.

He didn't have to say anything more. We had just spent two hours in the Musée Picasso and this was his conclusion: His daughter was no Picasso. Was no prodigy. I was twenty-six years old, and I was no Picasso.

"It will give you lifelong security." He looked directly at me, my features surely jumbled, certainly more distorted than any of the paintings we had just seen.

Mehry

2017

In moments of personal crisis, or sadness, or exhaustion, I crave the smell of saffron. When mixed with the steam from basmati rice, it sits in the air and will live in my hair. I catch whiffs of it on my clothing for days and buy saffron-infused oils to dab on my skin.

I think about this one weekend in the midst of caring for Amelia when I fly home to California for a quick visit—my mother's sister, my auntie Nargess, has arrived for a short trip from Iran. Within a couple of hours of takeoff, I am sitting on the floor of my parents' basement living room, surrounded by black-and-white photos and sifting through pictures from my mom's teenage years, her wedding to my father at the age of sixteen, and the early months after their arrival to the United States. A pot of rice bubbles on the stove and the smells of my mother's Persian cooking soothe my nerves.

"This is her, your mother, right?"

In my hand I hold a wallet-sized passport-style photo faded with crease lines around the edges. My mother is brewing tea and piling fruit in a bowl for my aunt, my uncle, and my dad.

"Yes, that's her."

I stare at the black-and-white face. A moon face. It is how we describe my mother's face: round and open and luminous. Cheekbones that create shadows in certain angles; wide-set brown eyes; thin, arched brows. Not the typical face of an Iranian. No large features, just porcelain-fair skin with a dainty nub for a nose, minimal cartilage, two symmetric nostrils peering up at the sky. The face in the photo is the face of my mother, but more serious, more tinged with sorrow. Less likely to burst into laughter or erupt with a smile the way my mother is prone to do. I hold the picture an arm's length from my own face.

"She was beautiful," I say out loud, and turn the photo around for my mother to see. Her hair is dark, also like my mother's, and falls in lines around the cheekbones, past her shoulders. From there, the image cuts off and her body is left to my imagination.

"Very beautiful," my mother answers. She pauses from serving tea and looks closely at the photo.

"Well, you look just like her," I say, and turn my face to my mother. The same face as in the photo. Just brighter. Alive.

My mom looks up at me, and I wonder what she sees. Not my grandmother's face, I know that. From very early I was aware that I took after my father, both in personality and in looks. Thick eyebrows spanning across a long nose. A dark and wicked sense of humor. A temper to be controlled. My mother existed in a different category from us. Angelic. Ethereal. Naturally pretty and mysterious. Less volatile. More nuanced.

"You are named after her, you know." My mother sits next to me on the floor and reaches for the photo.

"Fariba? My birth name?" I bring my grandmother's face back into my lap.

"No. Her name was Mehry. Like Mary. When we decided to change your name from Fariba, I wanted to call you Mary. After her."

I feel my mind swirl into confusion. My parents renamed me in 1979 when I started kindergarten in California. The Iran hostage crisis had captured the attention of the country. One night, over macaroni and cheese, as I was seated with my older brother, we learned that we were going to have new names. American names. I was no longer to be called Fariba—the name my mother said she knew before I was born. The name that would continue in the spirit of her own. She had been given the ancient Persian name Mahshid—Mah, for the moon; Shid, for light. Moonlight. She named my brother Farshid: sunlight. And she named me Fariba: charming, benevolent, enticing. To me it was a name that felt like more than just a name; it was a birthright.

"Wait, what?" I shake my head, close and open my eyes, and look again at the picture, at my mom. When I was renamed, I was named for my grandmother? This elusive being who floated in the background of my consciousness, who died in her twenties pregnant with her fifth child, whose life we never discuss?

"Yes, *dokhtaram*, daughter. I thought you knew that."

I take in a breath and slump my back into the couch. The day they changed our names our TV was a wooden-boxed behemoth that required four men to shift it two inches in order to lay down our newest Persian rug. Once the TV was in place, it was turned on and kept on one channel—ABC. Ted Koppel maintained a relentless position at the microphone.

The first day of the Iran hostage crisis is easy for me to remember—November 4, my mother's birthday. Around the world, every day to follow was counted in relation to that day: Day 5. Day 27. Day 100. The nation was haunted by the photos of young Americans bound and gagged, huddled in piles, marched through streets, blindfolded. The pictures were everywhere, and the pictures were terrifying. But that was over there. And now we are here. In California. Amid the safety of a beautiful new home, a cul-de-sac, walnut trees, and a creek.

We were a few months into the school year, and every day of kindergarten felt like an effort. I was too shy. Too scared. Too unfamiliar to blend right in. Was it just my nature, or did it have something to do with having left the United States as a toddler, spending eighteen months in Iran, and then returning to stay once we heard rumblings of a revolution? I did not mind the sitting and the working aspects of a kindergarten day, but recess and free play were a nightmare. I did not fit in.

"There are some nice girls in your class," my mother said to me in the morning, splashing water over my face and brushing my hair into high-on-my-head pigtails with bangs across my forehead, my favorite hairstyle, the one I wear in every picture from that year.

"The kids are mean," I answered. I watched my reflection in the bathroom mirror. I was seated on the bathroom vanity that I loved—a "Jack and Jill" bathroom with opposite sinks, a long counter, and mirrors on each side. Because of these mirrors my reflection was multiplied to infinity. My face bounced off in front of me, reflected behind me, and then continued in ever-shrinking size. For a shy five-year-old it was instant companionship. An opportunity to talk to a hundred faces. Me, and my many selves, perched and staring at one another over the years to come. My debrief space after school. My soliloquy audience. My tearful confessional. That mirror, those phantom heads, holding all my secrets.

"What makes them mean?" my mother asked, pausing from twisting plastic bands with colored stars to look at my face in the mirror, our reflection gaze safer than eye to eye. She waited, kept one hand on my back. I looked at her face and thought what I always thought when I looked at my mother—that she was the most beautiful woman I had ever seen. That her face was the perfect combination of sweet and pretty and caring and sad. That there was something in the way her dark hair fell past her shoulders with one strand stuck in her dimple that made me want to cry.

"Are the kids being mean to you?"

And that was what I could not and did not know how to explain. That it was not an overt meanness. That it was a subtle, secret taunting. That it was whispers. That it was fingers waggling out, ears and tongues sticking out when the teacher was not looking.

It was also what happened the day before as I walked back to my classroom from recess. Two second graders followed a third boy down the hall and out to the playground. Amir, dark and floppy-haired, wore a short-sleeved Izod shirt. He tried to ignore their calls, and I watched from my distant post. We were lined up, ready to march inside. Amir glanced over his shoulder, then turned his eyes to look ahead. I knew that look. I felt it in my cheeks, which froze in a pretend smile, and in my clenched teeth. Just keep walking, he might have thought, and I sent him similar signals. The entire class rounded the walkway and entered the open gates of our large concrete playground. It took just getting out of sight for the boys to approach him. I did not witness the attack, but I heard about it and imagined it forever.

"Towel-head," they called, and grabbed him by his wrists. One pinned his hands behind his back. "You are our hostage now," said the other, hitting him in the face.

I turned on my bottom away from the mirror and looked up into my mother's face.

"Kids hurt a boy in second grade," I told her. "Amir. They hit Amir."

My mother pressed me into her chest. My forehead lay against her body as she finished tying off my hair and held me with a rub of my back. She breathed and hugged me briefly, just enough, and then sat me back up.

"I will find out what happened." My mother spoke with a finality. "Don't worry about it. Don't worry about Amir. I will take care of it."

Just what "it" was I never truly discovered. I know that we never spoke of the incident again, but I watched my mother talk to the teachers that afternoon at pickup. I witnessed her putting an arm around Amir while she spoke in Farsi to his mom. I learned to keep my head down and my mouth shut about where my family came from. Nobody had to know.

"Your dad and I think it is time to pick out new names for you two," my mother said to us as we scooped spoons of baked macaroni into our mouths. My brother, still chewing, looked at me, his face a question mark. We were born only eleven months apart, so although he was the older one, he was also my Irish twin, and together—he with the deep thoughts, I with the mouth—we formed complete sentences. The kitchen was warm from the oven and the teakettle whistled. We ate while our mom added radishes and cucumbers to a green salad, mixed balsamic vinegar with spices for a dressing, and poured herself a weak cup of black tea with three sugar cubes. Our father was not yet home from work. Most nights he arrived just as we finished eating.

"What new name?" I poked my head up from decorating my fork with macaroni noodles, one noodle per prong, then put four at a time into my mouth.

"Easy names," she said. "Have you heard of the music group Peter, Paul and Mary?"

My brother and I shook our heads no, but this time, when he looked at me, it was with a smile. New names! the smile said. Finally!

"So, we are going to change Farshid to Peter, and Fariba to Mary." My mom's voice was gentle and sweet. She approached the table and sat between us at her spot, one end of the small rectangle. She was a youthful twenty-five-year-old with dark hair pulled into a loose ponytail. She delivered the news to us like no big deal, but her seat at the table, the way she paused to take in our expressions, told us she understood how we had been feeling like outsiders. That evening everything changed.

From there on out, we were no longer Iranian first. We had become Americans. Our new names would be the final piece of the puzzle connecting us to this place rather than Shiraz, the city we moved back to after our births. Peter and Mary would start school anew the next day, no longer foreigners with the names nobody could pronounce, but kids with the easiest, best, most popular names in the country. Peter and Mary. No more need for explanations. No more requirements to feel loyal to the place that kept showing up on the news. Peter and Mary could be as normal as we wanted to be. Fit in rather than stand out. Avoid confrontation. Erase judgment.

"Ha ha! Peter!" I pointed to my brother and laughed.

"I like Peter," he said. My mother pushed her chair back, picked up her cup of tea, and walked back toward the kitchen.

"Good," she said. "It is a beautiful name," she added.

I looked down at my fork, each prong naked now. The macaroni had gone cold, and I was not hungry anymore. Mary. I let the name swim in my mind. Mary. It's okay, I thought. Easy. And then it hit me. Mary!

"Can I be excused?" I was already out of my chair and headed toward my room before she could answer.

Where was it? I scanned my small bookshelf crammed with too many books, some facing out, others stacked. I was a reader—a big reader—and I had moved on to chapter books that year. But still, there were the favorites, the picture books with taped-up spines keeping them together.

"Found it!" I called, and ran back into the kitchen, a thin hardback book in my arms. It was the story of Rudolph the Red-Nosed Reindeer, an oversized Golden Book, my favorite of the Christmas stories for the lesson of the underdog and the magic of the elves.

On my knees, back at my seat, I opened the book and flipped the pages. My brother, now Peter, stood next to me, and my mother glanced over from the sink. I knew exactly the page I was looking for, two-thirds of the way in, and I turned and turned until I got to it.

"There!" I pointed.

And there it was. The page where Santa stands tall and, with one arm, unrolls his list. It is infinite in length, unfurled on the snow, and runs past the legs of the waiting reindeer. But his gloved hand holds it from the top edge. All the way down the page are the names of the good girls and boys, the ones who earned a visit from his sleigh. It is his big reveal, the one the North Pole has waited for all year. Who will they be? What are their names?

My brother and I spotted it at the same time. My finger pointed to the top of the list, the absolute top girl name on Santa's list. There it was: Mary. A bunch of names followed. Peter was there too, but much lower down. It was my name at the top. My new name. Mary.

I was giddy and lightheaded. It felt too good to be true. A new name. No more explanations. No more Fariba. And even better, there I was at the top of the list. The most worthy of all the children. Mary. I was meant to be.

I take one more look at my grandmother's photo and set it down in the pile.

"No," I say quietly, still shaking my head, remembering all the childhood years I felt a disconnect from our past, from my ancestry. "You never told me that about her name. I would have remembered."

I look up from my seat on the floor.

"Does anybody know why your mother died when she did?"

My father peers over his reading glasses, as always with a medical journal in his lap. Until I graduated from medical school in 2006, he had been the only doctor in the family for more than forty years. He always had the medical answers.

"I believe she had a stroke. High blood pressure in pregnancy," he says with a physician's confidence. I turn my head toward my mother and her sister, Nargess, seated on the couch together. My mother and uncle seem to nod in agreement with my father. But Nargess, with her bleach-blond hair in a braid and fingernails painted red, catches my eyes with hers and quietly shakes her head.

Does she know something we don't know? She is the only member of the family still living in my grandmother's city, Shiraz.

I raise my eyebrows back at her look and she puts her finger up to her nose, like a shush. I didn't imagine it. She knows.

Bolivia Mary

2018

The winter that followed my trip to California turned my hometown of Portland, Oregon, into a frozen tundra after weeks of ice, then snow, then rain that froze back to ice. The city felt under siege. School shut down for two weeks. Motorists abandoned vehicles on the freeway. I forgot what body temperature felt like. I needed my bone marrow to thaw.

Night after night I clicked through travelers' photos, searching for a spring break escape. I had not taken a vacation in more than a year. Babies kept coming. The midnight emergency tubal pregnancies and urgent patient phone calls never ceased. The ice storms simply made my work more difficult. I overnighted myself metal clips for my snow boots simply so I would be able to get off our slippery front porch, sometimes crawling on knees to the car to avoid a humiliating slide down the driveway. For a few days I couldn't leave the hospital and hunkered down in a windowless call room on the labor floor in case of a delivery. I felt trapped in my house, in the hospital, and in my own cycle of sleep deprivation and high expectations. I needed an out.

One night, scrolling through rental listings in Mexico, wrapped in hospital blankets and watching computer monitors click off fetal heart tracings, I found our tropical oasis.

"Just you guys staying here that week," the owner responded the next day by email. "You will have the pool, the hammocks, and the three-mile stretch of beach all to yourselves."

The idea of warmth, bare skin in the sunshine, saltwater lips, and long days lounging helped me endure the months that followed. My computer allowed escape into images of women in bright-colored bikinis, sarongs flowing down staircases that led to the ocean. That would be me. I closed my eyes night after night, still cold, the ice storm now a typical dark and wet infiltration under the surface layer of my skin. By March I was moldy on the outside but hopeful on the inside. I am a California girl, and I know the therapeutic effects of vitamin D. Glimpses in the mirror revealed a pale, tired doctor, mother, and wife, roles I alternated mechanically. I knew I was sufficiently good at each, but a thrill was missing. I did not know at the time how much I longed for a different version of myself.

Finally, spring break arrived and we disembarked outside a small Mexican airport. Sunlight hit our faces, and the kids squinted and squealed, throwing off their jackets before we made it to customs. I took a deep breath and turned my face toward the sun.

"Let's never leave," I said to Keith when we climbed into our rental car, soon arriving at our beachside oasis.

I quickly settled into a lounge chair facing the ocean and the kids jumped in and out of the swimming pool, looking as if they had just discovered water and warmth. Keith was already comfortable, sipping a beer and reading his book. I took in the crescent shape of the beach that we hovered above—clear tan sand, gentle waves, not another person in sight. I could happily stare at that view for days, fighting off every other thought. Worries from work crept in, like whether I closed the last patient's chart, whether I answered a phone call or looked at a lab result. It always took a couple of days to separate from the work. My breaks were riddled with anxiety about this pregnant patient or that surgical outcome. Occasionally, in the past, I might check in, pop on the computer, and make sure everybody was okay. But not here, I told myself. It had been forever since I separated myself from work, and I needed to let it go.

"Mama, get in! The water is perfect!" My daughter jumped to my side and my son called out. Swimming together was one of our favorite activities. They knew my love of being in the water, my tendency to jump into any pool, lake, river, or ocean.

"Eek! Okay . . ." I was roasting hot, and once my body hit the cool water all other thoughts disappeared. I squealed and laughed, swam with my daughter on my back, and dunked my son. A few minutes later I was back in my chair. I splayed myself, closed my eyes, and allowed sunrays to hit me. This feels perfect, I thought. This was just what I needed.

Looking back, I can see how the week worked into me like some sort of tropical spell. The more my legs tanned and my face freckled, the more I fell into old parts of me. I grew into my skin.

"I'm heading down to the ocean," I called to Keith while turning down the path to the beach.

"It's always great when you swim in the ocean," he answered back, swaying in a hammock, one leg dangling to the ground. "You look so happy."

That March, Keith and I were nearly ten years married. We had met serendipitously in an obscure town at the edge of the Amazon jungles of Bolivia. I was a medical student already looking for ways out of the mundane routine of medicine. Early one morning, I found myself searching for a place to check my email. It was 2005 and this required a small square room on the edge of town housing four computers. While dial-up internet buzzed, I chatted with my medical student buddy and then turned to my right.

Keith and I would argue about this detail: who arrived at the internet café first—me or him? I say I was there and he walked in. He insists he had been there when we entered. Either way, I looked three inches next to me and there was Keith, his stick-straight dark hair pointing skyward. He was tan with brown eyes and a prominent nose. I took an inhale. He was handsome. When he turned to look at me and words escaped his lips, I felt a momentary lightness pass through me. This I would not reveal to him for a very long time. But I will not deny, when he turned ninety degrees to face me, the words "I just met my husband" flashed across my mind.

Years after that meeting, Keith named the person he met in the internet café "Bolivia Mary." The thing with Bolivia Mary, he said, was the way she moved. Her hips swung separate from the rest of her body. Dyed blond hair down her back waving in one direction, head-tilting laugh thrown in the other. This was at the Octopussio nightclub at midnight. A twirl of bird bones spinning and dipping at the salsa dance club, her moves easy and quick. Her future husband had a glint in the eye and Bolivia Mary played it well. She felt like Beyoncé down there. Splurging on taxis to go out to dinner. Buying rounds of drinks for the table. She studied medicine and recited stories, spoke Spanish with patients by day and planned social events by night. Bolivia Mary—she killed it, learning-how-to-become-a-doctor with an attitude.

I forgot about her for years at a time. Keith and I would bring her up, but we talked about her like an old friend gone missing. Or deceased. She had been away for so long.

"Remember her laugh?" I would say to Keith in a longing way. "It came so easily."

"I remember her dance moves," Keith would answer. "That's when I knew I wanted her in my life."

We would sigh together, gaze at the ceiling above our couch, and listen to the children playing in their bedrooms.

The thing about being in Mexico, overlooking the waves of the Pacific Ocean, my swim cover off, the sun on my skin, was the way it reminded me of myself. A walk at sunrise with the sky turning from pink to blue, the brush of butterfly wings when one landed near my foot, the stars crowding the sky above my hammock. I felt her there—Bolivia Mary passed through me like a ghost. For just a second, she had been seen, and I knew what I had not known until then. She was still alive.

I shed my towel and hat and took my first dive into a wave. The salt in my mouth, the pressure over my head, was familiar from years of swimming in the ocean as a kid. I dove and rode small waves toward the sand. I flipped and backstroked out past a small cluster of breaker rocks where the sea became calm. I could spend all day out here, I thought, my hair radiating away from my head with the effect of a halo. This is what freedom feels like.

I shut my eyes, and my body bobbed and floated. I could not feel where my skin ended and the water began. Is there a moment when we awaken to our continuum? I only knew there was something about the sea seeping into the corners of my lips, the amniotic saline that tasted perfectly like tears. *Did you feel it when you left us?* I stared at the wisp of a cloud above me, my foot anchored on a rock to keep me in one spot as the waves lulled me, trancelike. *Mehry*. My grandmother's life pulsed just underneath my skin and now, in what felt like the connectivity of water and sky and present and past, she appeared. Her story was the story I needed to know. It unfolded in the lapses between the whitecaps, and I could finally see her, like this:

The family lives in Shiraz, Iran. It is 1956. I do not know the temperature on that exact day, or the names that belong to all of the faces. I do not know the precise aroma that travels from the back of the kitchen to the bedrooms in the front. The sounds are muffled in my mind. The details are made up, but the details are critical. I want to re-create that day. I want to reimagine my history. This is the year my grandmother dies. This is the only fact that is clear.

Mehry is a languishing twenty-six years old. A few years earlier the word used to describe her would have been *Zeebah*, in the Persian language. Glowing. Beautiful. Radiant. As the babies come, a layer of youthful sheen shimmers off. She does not lose her beauty, but, as with many women burdened by the weight of pregnancies, births, infant care, and household, the beauty transfers. Sparkles of light bounce from her into the glowing brown eyes of her children. Her smooth skin rubs off when the two-year-old, the four-year-old, the five-year-old, and the baby are bathed and lotioned. She holds their bellies to her face and breathes. As her cheek rests on their bodies, invisible slivers of herself remain behind. Layers come off. She senses that she is becoming slowly exposed. And she is pregnant again.

She has not yet told anybody and has not seen the doctor. But after four pregnancies, four babies, there is no doubt. First came the headaches and the turning of her stomach. Food smells repelled her and sent her running to the bathroom. She feels the fatigue of early pregnancy, the extraordinary needs of a one-centimeter fetus building a heart, brain, spinal cord, genitalia. She marvels that nothing is consciously required of her to create this new life. Only her vital energy sources are needed—blood, food, air—and yet this time around, she finds it so difficult.

She takes a step into the kitchen, hugging her cotton robe closer to her body. Here, in Shiraz, the seasons transition from summer to fall with a dramatic chill. Her toes hit the tiled floor and she winces from the cold. No going back to the bedroom for slippers now. The baby is sure to wake with one more sound of her steps. She turns the gas knob with a *click-click-click* to warm water for her tea, feels her skin begin to warm from the heat.

She closes her eyes, holds a tin to her nose, and breathes in the fragrance of black tea—pungent and raw. Darjeeling, imported from India. This is what she wakes for. She pours the tea leaves into the bottom of her porcelain teapot, white with a rose painted on its side. Today might be the day to add dried orange flowers. Some days it is rose water, other times cardamom. But with her stomach turning she imagines it is time for orange flowers, picked last spring from the citrus trees that line the house. Waxy leaves and white, fragrant flowers handed to her in a basket by the gardener.

Her son Mansour watches her from the kitchen doorway, anticipating the smile she will put on for him. She will ignore her nausea, erase her headache, and reach for his head of hair, which she will run her fingers through before pulling him to her belly for a kiss on the forehead.

"*Khoob-ee?*" Are you good? she asks. She worries about this new baby inside, and she worries about this son. Getting so big, she thinks, brushing a bread crumb off his cheek.

They sip their tea together. He decided he was old enough to start drinking the dark tea, and he balances a sugar cube in between his teeth, the way he has seen the men do. Hot liquid flows through the cube, saccharine sweetness melting all over his tongue. Warm and sweet, the most delicious sensation. (As it happens, he will always love sugar. And caffeine. He will need this moment to replay itself. Forever.)

Her younger daughter, Nargess, toddles in. The two-year-old is fussy and will become feisty. She has crawled out of her crib again and runs down the hall, eager to get into the kitchen, where the floor is warmer from the oven and where she knows her mother will scoop her up into her arms. Her short hair smells of soap and pillow, and she smiles, opens her arms wide when she sees her mother seated in the chair. Her mother cannot help but smile back. An invisible charge runs between them, and the toddler injects her mother with enough voltage to get her through the next few hours. This is motherhood, Mehry thinks. Down one moment, up the next.

The four-year-old has not walked into the kitchen yet. She has been awake the longest but waits quietly in her bedroom. She likes to pretend she is asleep when the others are awake. She finds comfort in listening to the household slowly emerge from slumber. The four-year-old stays under the cover of her wool blanket, pulls it up over her nose to feel her breath warm her entire body. She does not want to miss the baby's cry. She will be the first in the room to greet him. The baby will hear her voice first, a high-pitched bell announcing that help is on its way, a songbird chirping its morning hello.

"*Ghereh-nakon, ghereh-nakon.*" Don't cry, don't you cry, she will sing her made-up melody, a slightly different tune every day.

This is the part where the four-year-old picks up the baby, nestles him on her lap, allows her hair to fall onto his body, cups her nose and mouth with a hand, and breathes her warm air down his shirt. This calms him and delights him. He smiles. He giggles. They rock together. The four-year-old thinks of herself as a mother and the scene plays in my head. I can see her. I cannot see her. She is my mother. I know what happens and even though I am watching now, a part of me wants to look away.

I don't know how long I spent in the water. My grandmother's story faded quickly, like waking from a dream. I emerged with wrinkled toes facing an expanse of hard, smooth sand, a palette of the outgoing tide. Glancing up the cliff, I could see my family still up by the pool. I turned my attention to the beach, the sea and its held history behind me. I was back on the earth and this was cartwheel sand, I thought, staring at the miles of perfectly flat, firm ground. It had been a while since I had done a cartwheel, but there were years in my childhood and into my twenties when I would not pass a flat piece of lawn or beach without kicking upside down.

I went for it and stood tall after the first cartwheel. I tried to disregard anybody watching from above, but I knew myself—I was a sucker for an audience. I straightened my legs and pointed my toes. Blood rushed out of my head into my feet, and I ignored the dizzy feeling that followed. I used to do twenty of these in a row, back and forth across the gym. I kicked up again. Number two, then number three. Feeling a little woozy, I threw myself into the fourth and there, midway, with my legs in the air and my hair touching the earth, my fortysomething self greeted my twenty-two-year-old self.

"Hello," I said, admiring her slim figure and confident smile.

"You're still cartwheeling?" she answered back, not judging but curious.

"I took a break for a while," I answered, feeling high, a sort of euphoria expanding my chest. "But I think I'm back." I landed left foot, right foot, and threw my arms straight to the sky like an Olympian.

The Size of a Human Heart

2018

The fading tan after Mexico hurt almost as much as a persistent throb in the back of my left leg from the cartwheels. I felt a layer of sunshine shed from my skin the minute I entered the hospital the following week. The locker-room reflection of me getting ready for a long shift, dressed in blue scrubs, my hospital ID tag around my neck, and my phone clipped to my waistband confirmed that I was back in uniform. Are you in there, Bolivia Mary? I squinted and pushed my face closer into the glass. I faked a smile and considered keeping my hair down in beachy waves. Ugh, I sighed, and swept it into a messy bun at the top of my head.

I went through the motions of rounding on new mothers, exclaiming over newborn feet, and checking in on the ones still in labor. It felt not so different from returning to morning rounds nearly a decade earlier, when I reentered the grueling hours of ob-gyn residency eight weeks after delivering my son via C-section.

Those mornings my alarm clock woke me at five o'clock to allow time for me to pump breast milk. I would sneak one last look at my newborn, snapping flash-free photos, before tiptoeing out of the room to face a punishing twenty-four-hour shift. Despite having put our lives on hold through medical school and entering residency in our late twenties to mid-thirties, no ob-gyn resident in my program had chosen to have a baby during those four years of training—I was a first. It was not a planned pregnancy after six months of dating Keith, but a pregnancy that happened despite precautions and birth control and, clearly, a knowledge of fertility windows and ovulation. Discovering I was pregnant brought expected panic—I was working nearly a hundred hours a week and had three more years to go. But also, I was thirty-two years old, and there was nothing, truly nothing, I wanted more than to be a mother.

Telling my parents the news was terrifying. And when they flew across the country to watch us get married, my father insisting on it eighteen weeks into my pregnancy, I relented. It felt like casting shame onto our traditional family values to stay unmarried and pregnant, and so I buried any resistance to the idea and didn't fight him. We planned a wedding ceremony in four days, and on a drizzly hillside overlooking Cape Cod, with a small bump underneath my sundress, the sun broke through clouds, my father gave an emotional speech to the six of us present, and a double rainbow appeared in the sky.

I was met with quiet resignation by my program administrators when I promised to stay extra in the evenings in order to take several fifteen-minute milk-pump breaks during the day. I agreed not to take another day off for two and a half years to make up my maternity leave time, and I worked an extra month in the summer after my classmates had graduated even though my son was by then a toddler. I pretended not to hear when older doctors discussed my return to work after eight weeks.

"Something seems different about her now," I overheard them say. As if the baby I left each morning with his father was not an expression of every blood cell in my body. As if his head was not the perfect size of a human heart.

I squeezed my eyes closed and then opened them again as if to physically reset the memories of the early days of training with a newborn—even after more than a decade, it felt as if the stress of those years still resided just under my skin. As soon as I settled into a desk on the labor floor to chart on the computer, I was called into a triage room.

"Doctor!" A nurse poked her head out the door, motioning toward me. A mother of identical twins had come into the hospital worrying that she had not felt the babies move all day. I moved into rapid motion. I knew that in these situations, seconds and minutes can be the difference between losing and saving not just one but two babies. After just a few minutes of watching, the heart rate tracing alerted us that the twins were in trouble. This was where the team mattered. Within seconds of my looking up at the nurse with the words "We have to go," the unit activated. The operating room designated for C-sections across the hall was lit, packets of sterile instruments were broken open and splayed across the table. I called out for an assistant, with one hand guiding the rolling bed that the mother lay on as a nurse pushed her toward the OR doors.

She was, obviously, terrified. Within five minutes of arriving on our unit, we were telling her that the babies would be born now. There was no time for an epidural or spinal anesthesia. She would be put to sleep and only when she woke up forty-five minutes later would she know the fate of her babies.

She had carried these babies for thirty-four weeks. This came after years of infertility, attempts to get pregnant, miscarriages, and grief, I learned later. When she finally became pregnant her entire community mobilized to support her family. Church congregations prayed for the babies' safe arrival. Grandparents knit blankets and hats. To create identical twins is a miraculous feat of split cells and shared DNA that evolve into matching noses and holiday outfits. Movies are made and scientific papers written about the unlikely separation and reuniting of twins who are raised in opposing environments but still share a propensity for classical music or both end up as luxury car mechanics.

None of these thoughts entered my head as I washed my hands and allowed a scrub tech to throw a sterile gown over my body. Another doctor joined me and the two of us made quick work of delivering the babies. In an emergency, the time between a scalpel on the skin and delivering a baby can be under a minute. We simply place our fingers within the open skin surface, break and stretch fascia, muscle, and peritoneum until we get to the muscle wall of the uterus. One quick splice and the first baby joined the growing team in the room—resuscitation nurses, respiratory therapists, anesthesia, more nurses. Our patient's husband was waiting outside the operating room doors, since this case was too emergent and the patient was being put to sleep. We were aware that he would be escorted to the NICU (neonatal intensive care unit) as soon as the first twin was whisked away. Their team, just on the other side of a door, had set up side-by-side warmers. A neonatal pediatrician arrived, and they all murmured hurried instructions to each other as they waited.

The first baby was large. Its face, arms, and belly were swollen, engorged with extra fluid that also burst from the amniotic sac and flooded the floor beneath us. She was not crying, but there was a heartbeat. We clamped the umbilical cord and handed her to a nurse waiting with a warm blanket. They exited the room and within seconds, her sister was delivered. She was the antithesis of the first baby—emaciated, skin and bones. There was such little fluid around her I was forced to peel the membranes of the amniotic sac off her delicate skin in order to cut and clamp the umbilical cord.

"She was vacuum sealed," I said to my partner across from me. This sister was silent, barely moving, but also with a heartbeat. We gently placed her in the second set of warm-blanket arms and watched her get moved next door.

When identical twins are forced to share the lifeblood of one placenta, a creeping imbalance can arise within the uterus. The maze of vessels used to feed each one its fair share of fluid, blood, and nutrients might lose its way and shunt entirely toward one baby and away from the other. It is called twin-to-twin transfusion syndrome (TTTS). The life pouring into one deprives the other one. Common sense makes us think that the little one, the dry one, the stuck twin, would fare worse. But this is the one who more often survives. The stress of deprivation increases survival—the hormone cortisol is secreted in higher amounts and it stimulates a fight for life in this frail but feisty baby. The abundant one, the inadvertent receiver, this is the one more likely to die.

The room hushed to barely a sound as we did the work of sewing the mom back together. Judging by the way they looked, all of us knew that both of the babies had little chance of survival. The surgery ended unceremoniously. The mother was awakened, so groggy she could barely comprehend what was happening.

"The babies, my babies?" she asked as she looked up, before shutting her eyes again and falling back to sleep. I exited the room, changed out of my messy scrubs, placed orders on the computer, and poured myself a cup of ice water. The mother would go to recovery and do fine. I peeked in the window and could see the babies were being cared for by experts in the NICU, each bed surrounded. There was nothing more for me to do but wait. I lay on the firm twin bed in my call room, a tiny windowless space identical to every call room I had ever known. I felt my muscles relax as the adrenaline from the past hour started to leave my body. What if she hadn't come in, I wondered, at just that time? What if the team had not been prepared and able to act so quickly?

My eyelids closed and I entered a half-dream state, my pager still pressed against my waist in case I was called to another emergency. Hospital naps were always strange, as sleeping while remaining vigilant is not a natural state. My mind drifted back to Mexico, to how it felt to remember the old parts of myself.

What was it about Bolivia Mary? For one thing, she seemed fearless. After two weeks working in the clinics and hospitals of the capital city of La Paz, she asked to be transferred to the jungle. She wanted to see how medicine was practiced where all the modernities of medicine had not yet infiltrated. She ended up on the outskirts of the Amazon, within the walls of a clinic with an ob-gyn who had trained overseas and was back to serve his community.

In those days, birth control was illegal in Bolivia, as was abortion. Cultural machismo prevented the men from wearing condoms and one after another women were birthing two, four, six, twelve babies. Due to illness, malnutrition, infection, many children did not survive and the mothers bore the physical and emotional toll of these families.

The doctor in the rural jungle clinic closed the shades when his patients entered his office. He was a quiet man, but friendly. He spoke to me mostly under his breath, about not writing anything down, about not asking their names. From inside their purses, women pulled out boxes of IUDs they had purchased off the black market, on the streets, or from friends. These appointments were mostly silent, as each player knew their role—hand the box to the ob-gyn, undress and place feet in stirrups, clench teeth as the IUD was inserted, nod when the doctor trimmed the strings short enough so that no husband could feel them, place the empty box back into the purse, and leave the office without a trace.

Up until that clinic experience, I was in Bolivia to train to become a pediatrician. I loved children more than anything and knew I wanted to care for them personally and professionally. After eight hours witnessing the exchange between this doctor and the women of his community, I changed my mind and never turned back. When the mothers are cared for, the families are safer. When the mothers have agency, their children are more likely to thrive.

A couple of hours after the C-section, while the babies were in the NICU, I visited the mother in her room. She was still recovering and had not yet been able to see her twins.

“I know they are going to be okay.” She smiled and nodded.

Her mother, the grandmother, nodded in agreement. "We have a strong faith," she added. "They are going to be okay."

I sat on the end of the bed, wanting to feel optimistic with them. I knew that outcomes were not always as we hoped and that the best people sometimes ended up with the worst grief. I smiled, and with my hands on my patient's legs, I nodded and reiterated that their faith and hope and belief were necessary and powerful. In my head, I relived the scenes from the delivery. The first baby, engorged with fluid, its cheeks round and Buddha-like. The second baby, barely moving, emaciated and dry. I knew the statistics in these cases. But I did not paint this picture for the believers in the room. I knew that what I said in that moment held weight, that the role I played right now was soothsayer. I had been in this position long enough to understand that my words held power, they would be repeated via text and over the phone as prophecy. In a tenuous life-and-death situation where my actual power was limited, I carefully chose what I said.

"They are beautiful." I squeezed the mother's foot through a blanket. "And strong. Little fighters."

I passed the NICU more than a dozen times that day. Through the window blinds I could not see the twins because each bed was surrounded by working bodies—the pediatrician, the respiratory therapists, a team of nurses. The father of the babies walked between the beds, bent over, quietly listening to what was being said about their conditions.

As the day progressed, I remembered how Bolivia Mary also rode a nighttime refurbished ambulance around the Amazon jungle doing community house calls. Every evening, after a day in the hospital clinic, she met a different team at the village public health hut to plan the visits for that night. Inside the rustic concrete building, a large sheet of white butcher paper was pinned to the wall, colored markers labeling every road and house in the village. Sticky notes indicated who lived inside: "17 yrs old, pregnant, due date Dec," "Active tuberculosis, needs meds," "Newborn April, vaccines," and so on. We had coolers holding polio vaccines in droplets, prenatal vitamins, prescription medication, and each night we set out to visit the homes, weigh the babies, listen to lungs, distribute the meds.

The pediatrician did not leave the NICU that day, nor that night. I don't believe she ever sat down, not from the moment we handed her both babies. She was twenty-three hours into her shift when they decided to fly the sisters to a university hospital for an even higher level of care. When they were stable enough to make the flight, nurses strapped the preemies into beds like miniature pilots heading off on the mission of their lives. The pediatrician later said that she and her team had never retrieved two babies from the brink of death so many times. Over and over again, over the course of the day and into the night, they thought they were losing both, and miraculously, each kept returning back to life.

The emergency delivery of the twins reawakened an understanding of something inside me that had been missing for a while—access to high-quality medical care made a real difference. This had been obvious to Bolivia Mary, but the day-in, day-out demands of medical training, battling insurance companies, fighting for time with patients had dimmed my own perspective. Getting caught up in the DHS fights for Amelia, feeling like there was no end to the obstacles we faced in providing patients with what they needed. But the jungle ob-gyn had created a birth control option for mothers. The nighttime ambulance team figured a way to work around the limitations of transportation to provide lifesaving medicine.

The little twin recovered more quickly. The receiver twin, the big one, got everything in utero. The red blood cells. The potassium. The space to move freely. But it was the starved twin, the depleted one, who used all her remaining strength. Her lungs responded to all the therapies, the oxygen and medication. She settled into her temporary life support while her sister—the chunky one with the cheeks and the thigh fat—had to fight harder. In the end, their mother was right. They both survived. A mere three weeks after we nearly lost them, they were buckled into car seats, taking a victory lap home. Sometimes the depleted one, she surprises us.

Hammam

2018

Knowing that Mehry had died while pregnant changed my relationship to my job, my patients, the purpose of my career. She was a haunting I couldn't escape because day after day, I was faced with other mothers, other pregnancies, and the interplay between their conditions and my profession. Mehry haunted me. But then it occurred to me: I didn't know anything about my father's mother, only that she too had left the family at a young age. One evening, I called my dad and asked him to tell me what happened to my other grandmother, Afsar.

"When I was twelve years old, I was handed my newborn baby sister wrapped in a blanket, put into the back of a taxi, and instructed to go to the police station and tell them we had found a baby on the sidewalk."

He cleared his throat, and my eyes stung with surprised tears. I had never heard this story.

"The police asked if it was a boy or girl." My father nodded his head and remembered. "We said, 'How would we know?' They knew we were lying but took the baby from us anyway."

After that day, my father never saw his sister again. He returned to the apartment building; his mother was also gone, having been admitted to a psychiatric hospital and never returned again to the family.

He described his mom, Afsar, as a quiet woman, a depressed woman who spent most days staring out the window of their concrete, electricity-less housing complex outside of Tehran. Apparently, shortly after the birth of her fourth infant, she had a psychotic break. How this presented is still not entirely clear, but I can imagine. After nearly a decade of caring for postpartum mothers, I knew how the chemical changes of the postpartum period could invade even the most highly functional brains. Blank faces, absent looks, intrusive thoughts, unnerving anxiety, detachment—they had all walked into my clinic doors. Some of these mothers imagined hurting the baby they so desperately wanted. Others could not shake the idea that something sinister was going to happen to the child. One undressed completely and stood naked in the middle of the road, where her husband found her, guided her inside, and called my clinic right away.

My father told me he was sent away shortly after his mother, raised by his aunt with his cousins. His father quickly remarried, and more children were born; there was simply no way to take care of them all. It was my father's intellect and determination that transformed his life from essentially that of an orphan to the top medical student in his class, and then to a recruit at the Johns Hopkins University School of Medicine in America. In his twenties, his motherless self met my mom's motherless self and together they set off to create a new kind of life for each other and for their children.

Learning that my grandmothers had both been lost to obstetric complications softened me toward the decision I had made years before to become a doctor. The process of applying to medical school, passing multiple exams, surviving the grueling hours of residency training, and accumulating debt is not for the ambivalent or unenthusiastic. I put it off for years. Perhaps I didn't want to feel like I was "doing it for my father." Maybe I feared losing my free-spirited ways. Nearly ten years into my career, catapulting toward exhaustion, burning out from overnight shifts and administrative demands, confronting policy changes that dictated how we practiced medicine, I thought my ambivalence had probably been justified.

But then, Mehry became pregnant again. Not in my lifetime, but it might as well have been. Because her pregnancy consumed me. I wanted to know what happened, and when I asked her, she wove a story in my head. It confused me at first—what was real, and what was imagined.

"Does it matter?" she answered me one day. "Just pay attention. You will figure it out."

The women talked, she tells me, and I focus on her voice.

They talked all the time, I hear her say. The women talked at the spot between their houses, where courtyard walls ended in air and road, forked boundaries between their public and private lives. They talked when they paused at the grocers, holding canvas bags of feta cheese and chicken thighs in their arms. Their voices rang over the hum of the water kettle, across rooms, in the yard against concrete walls. They arranged routines around their conversation. They underwent weekly excursions to the bathhouse, the hammam—a ruse for a half day of gossip. The women would sit with their feet in the crystal waters, two by two, or in larger groups standing in a circle, the pools absorbing their words. Dissecting expressions. Worrying about their children. Discussing the men. Questioning politicians. Laughing. Crying. Plucking. Shaving. Exfoliating. Scrubbing. And talking, talking, talking.

Mehry was the quiet one. She kept her thoughts to herself and limited her words. She entered the hammam every week, yearned to find an empty spot in the corner of the steamy room where she could slip off her clothing and bathe solo. She limited her talk to the workers who clamored to wash her hair. Because she was not picky and tipped well, they offered to scrub the dead off her skin. She had porcelain cheeks and long, thick hair that sheened and glowed after a good rinsing.

The day after Mehry realized she was pregnant—again—she ventured to the hammam a day earlier than usual, with hopes that the steam and the waters would settle her stomach and comfort her nerves. She had told no one.

"Salaam, salaam." She nodded a hello to the *amehs*, the elder aunties who sat vigil in their usual spot near the entry. Two of them sat on stone steps covered by towels, their heads damp and drying. Different day, different aunties, but always the same routine.

"That new young bride," one clucked, and pointed with a nod of her head.

Mehry looked toward the object of their gaze, a beautiful young girl with dark hair and emerald-green eyes, seated with friends at the edge of the largest pool.

"Firm breasts, but wide hips," the other said, and shook her head sadly.

"Will only get wider after the babies," the first replied. "Poor thing."

"She is not the poor thing!" number two exclaimed. "Her husband. He will have to feed all the children, and those hips!"

Although she knew her pregnancy was early and her stomach unchanged, she figured the aunties would discern her condition quickly. She did not know how they did it, but they always knew—either from the greenish hue of her cheeks, the slight fullness of her lips, or perhaps her nipples, which were already darkening. They predicted her pregnancies every time, sometimes before even she knew. With the first three, Mansour, Mahshid, and Nargess, they clicked their tongues and cautioned her to avoid the lavender scrub. With Mohsen, the baby, they looked almost sympathetic, as if they knew the feeling of carrying a fourth so quickly after the first three. They whispered among themselves that her face looked weary. That Mr. Abedi, her husband, though charming and handsome, needed to give her a break.

Mehry undressed in her private space and an attendant helped slip plastic slippers on her feet. The main room was a sanctuary of steam and hot tea, chatter, and camaraderie, each stone pillar ending in a crescent-shaped arch, gracing the tall ceilings. Fountains of blue reflecting the colors of mosaic-tiled ceilings above:

turquoise, yellow, and green. An occasional young child rested with a head on her mother's lap. Some of the younger women lounged in robes, their heads wrapped in towels. Others bathed in the nude, slim figures sprawled on carpets, sipping tea.

Mehry found her place at the pool opposite the aunties. While they might still talk about her, at least this way she could be spared the details.

Her attendant helped her untie her robe, placed a dab of cucumber-scented face cream on her cheeks and forehead, then disappeared. Mehry stepped her toes in first, then sank down to her waist in the room-temperature water. It was perfect. She and the water, a continuum. It was what she loved best about floating in this pool—the feeling that she did not exist apart. The sensation that her body was simply a vessel to contain within her a version of the same water.

She closed her eyes, and the buoyancy of her body released the ropy tension within her arms, her legs, and now her belly. Deep breaths, she told herself. Breathe in through your nose, out through your mouth, something she remembered her grandmother saying to her as a child as she tried to fall asleep, always fitful, always nervous. Slowly, slowly, with her arms by her sides, hair flowing like a halo, she let go of the thoughts that kept her awake at night. The wondering about her future. The empty absence of her husband in their bed, around just long enough for another baby. The despair over her loneliness.

"*Mehry, Mehry jan, tow ee?*" Mehry, dear, is that you?

She felt a tickle on the bottom of her right foot and then her big toe being tugged.

Mehry startled back into the room.

"Nilufar, salaam." Mehry's legs floated down from the water's surface and her toes tapped the sandpaper-textured floor of the pool. Her head hung back, weighed down by her length of wet hair. She twisted it, damp and tangled, into a loose bun as she stood up.

A young woman, her own hair cut in an asymmetric bob, bounced up and down in front of her.

"Mehry, it is you!" She grabbed Mehry's face in her hands, kissed each cheek, then leaned back to take a long look.

"Poor thing. You do look tired," she said as she tilted and nodded her head, as if she had overheard the aunties talking. "Is everything okay?"

"Okay?" Mehry blinked. "Yes, yes, of course, everything is good, I'm good."

Nilufar stood in front of her, her breasts barely submerged, her bony shoulders rising and falling with the gentle lapping of water. Her lipstick was dark red, creamy, and each eyebrow a perfect brushstroke line. Nilu, a friend of the family from childhood, impish and sweet. She had also married young, but her husband worked in town, a teaching job at the university. They stopped having children after their two daughters. How long had it been since she and Nilu had spoken? At a cousin's wedding several years ago? At Mehry's wedding a few years before that?

Two attendants placed cloths on the edge and draped warmed towels around their shoulders. Mehry was grateful for the coverage. Despite a lifetime of public bathing, sitting and talking in the nude always made her uncomfortable. She hugged the towel over her shoulders, covered her sagging belly. She felt bread and cheese from her breakfast rise within her and placed a hand on her sternum.

"How is Ali Agha, Mr. Ali, your husband? And the kids? They must be growing," Mehry said to Nilu, who leaned back on her hands, her body arched, a towel laid across her lap. Nilu let out a big sigh.

"Good, good, they are all good. You know, the usual. Work. School. Family. We are blessed."

Mehry forced a smile, her head nodding, her eyes heavy. This was exactly what she tried to avoid when coming to the hammam. This small talk. This running into acquaintances. It was why, when the hammam had become too much of a place of inquiry, she had switched the day of her weekly visit in the first place. Ladies from her past approached her with questions, concern. She was looking too thin, her face looked pale, her hair looked limp. No end to their observations. One day, in between her first two pregnancies, she paused to say a polite hello to the aunties. One had reached out and pinched her waist, dragging her hand slowly over her backside.

"Getting fat, huh?" the auntie had said curtly, and then laughed. An expected intrusion, a violation she had grown up with. This eyeballing and judging. This frankness. In a culture where men and women remained separate until their wedding night, the women served as purveyors of one another's bodies. Older ladies watched the younger ones, slyly felt their curves, their skin, and reported back to their sons, their nephews.

So, she had switched her day. And since then, she grew more and more anonymous. The other women eventually understood it was best to leave her alone.

"That Mehry," they would say to one another. "Poor thing just seems tired."

"Such a beauty," they would whisper. "But with misery, even beauty fades."

Mehry looked down and felt the top of her hand being stroked gently by Nilu's thumb, the nail perfectly filed. An unconscious move that a mother makes when she holds a child's hand, reassuring, caring. It was enough, just enough, to allow her shoulders to relax.

"So, how are you, Mehry, dear? How is your husband?"

For a moment, Mehry thought she might just tell her everything. Describe the empty corners of the house. Explain how quiet it was at night after the children were asleep. When her husband was out of town. Sometimes for days, sometimes for weeks. She might tell Nilu that she never fell asleep completely, that she turned and rolled, walked the courtyard, and read books to herself all throughout the night. She waited for morning. She wanted to tell Nilu that everything had changed. The exuberance she had felt when she was first married, the joy at the arrival of each baby, was fading. That her kids were the only bright spots in the house and in her thoughts. That her husband was no longer around. And that when he was, their exchanges were brief and reflexive. They slept together less and less. And when they did, she no longer felt his desire for her. Nilu's thumb stroked one, two, three, and with each stroke Mehry imagined a confession. She knew the marriage had been arranged. Stroke. She knew it was her father's dying wish. Stroke. She loved her husband but questioned his love for her. Stroke. She was pregnant again. Stroke. She had her own desires. Stroke. She felt a stirring within. Stroke. Stroke. There had to be more for her in this world. Stroke. She knew nothing of her own heart. Stroke. Stroke. Stroke. Stroke.

"Can I ask you a question, Nilu?" She spoke while looking straight ahead.

"Of course, anything."

"Did you ever want more than two children?" Mehry formed the words carefully. She was surprised by Nilu's laugh in response.

"More than two children?! Never. Of course not. Don't you think if I wanted more than two children, I would have more?" She asked the question as if the answer was obvious.

"So then . . . how . . . ?" Mehry stopped her sentence when she looked at Nilu's face. Nilu immediately turned serious.

"Mehry. Are you saying that you don't know how to stop yourself from having babies?" Her hand reached out again, and she grabbed Mehry's hand, her thumb stroking the top of her knuckles. "You know that there are ways to not have babies, right?" She asked the question again because Mehry's body froze. Only her neck could move, and it twitched back and forth.

"Are you pregnant again?"

Mehry's neck managed a tiny nod.

"I knew it," Nilu sighed. "So tired. You must be so tired."

Mehry nodded again, just a little, her eyes stinging with the wet feeling.

"Ali and I," Nilu started. "Well, Ali and I have gotten very good at knowing when to not have, you know, relations."

Mehry turned and looked at her friend. Was she saying this was something she talked about with her husband?

"And the couple of times I did get pregnant after having our children . . ." Nilu continued, and Mehry tried to keep her expression straight. "Well, we took care of it."

Mehry felt her entire being melt into her robe. Nilu understood. She closed her eyes, letting go of a tear that dropped out of each. She was, she felt, finally not alone.

"I can help you," Nilu started. "Come back next week. I will have for you what you need."

Planter Boxes

2018

I spent much of my late twenties working for a nonprofit institute specializing in improving public health. My favorite project involved researching how to best care for elderly patients in nursing homes. We visited long-term residential homes to consider how they were designed, and interviewed people who worked and lived there. Our research led us to one facility with rolling gardens on wheels—planter boxes that could be moved to residents who were confined to wheelchairs or beds.

Putting fingers in the dirt, it turned out, helped lift the patients' moods. Nurturing and growing plants also triggered memories from their pasts, and stories began to emerge from childhood. Some patients found themselves sharing stories, the distant look in their eyes replaced with something more alive.

During one nursing home visit, I sat with one of the residents while he used a stick to create a mini-irrigation system around a row of marigolds.

"My wife loved to garden," he shared with me in a quiet voice, our gaze focused on the stick tracing circles around the flowers. "We were married for forty-five years."

I picked a few dry petals off a zinnia and suddenly I was back on that bench in Paris with my father, both of us staring at the perfectly curated garden. "You're no Picasso." I could still hear those words in his voice.

"I like having my hands in the dirt too," I replied, digging a little hole with my fingers to place the next potted plant.

I enjoyed my work at the nonprofit, but I often found myself contemplating medical school. It was what had been expected of me, and so I had been resistant to it. But I was not completely satisfied in my current role. I spent much of my time at a desk in front of a computer. If what I wanted was dirt under my fingernails, then perhaps practicing medicine *was* the answer. The possibility of truly changing people's health and lives. The one-on-one conversations. The chance to look somebody in the eye when I asked them questions. The one who broke the bad news, but with one hand on a knee, face-to-face, assuring that everything would be okay. I could almost imagine myself poring over lab results and radiology reports, coming up with a long-awaited diagnosis and plan. What if, one day, people knew me as "doctor," with affection in their voices?

It was not an overnight decision but a gradual reckoning, simmering over time. Once our project at the nursing home ended, I gave my notice, and within a month, I had submitted my application to medical school.

Now, twenty years later, I knew that my decision to become a doctor was the right one. I was the first touch in the world for thousands of babies, I had built a community practice for entire families, my patients hugged me in grocery stores and on airplanes, and I could tick off surgery successes, cancer diagnoses caught early, and patients who felt seen. But I also could no longer deny that the system was broken, that our medical model made giving and receiving high-quality care nearly impossible for many. I also could no longer deny that the systemic obstacles were slowly wearing everybody down—the patients, the healthcare workers, and me.

Many doctors choose to leave their careers when burnout kicks in. Others succumb to depression or substance abuse. Suicide deaths are up to four hundred percent higher among female physicians when compared to women in other professions. I knew the statistics and I knew that I did not want any of that for myself. What if, I began to daydream, I could reimagine the way I did my job? What if, twenty years into my medical career, what I needed was more dirt. New seeds. A knuckling in the soil.

Part Two

Mobile Clinic

2022

I pulled my car in front of the gate of the parking lot that housed the RV. It was pouring, which meant I would have to unlock the chain, roll the gates open, back out the thirty-one-foot vehicle, and leave it in the road with blinking emergency lights on—while I drove my own car in; transferred equipment, supplies, and laundry; then locked the gates closed again, all in a Portland rainstorm. From inception to execution, no part of my new business was easy.

Prior to walking into Camping World the year before, wearing a faux fur coat and pearls, to sign the paperwork on the RV I had selected, I spent nearly a year planning. I convinced my malpractice insurance to provide coverage for my unique model of care with articles about shortages of ob-gyns clipped from *The New York Times*. I did not have funding, nor much money, and I did not know exactly where we would park, how we would schedule patients, or whether we could generate enough revenue to survive. But there were a few things I did know: I knew how to run a private medical practice—I had been doing that for nearly a decade. I knew how to care for patients and how to build trust within my community. I knew that most of the things I needed to perform a medical exam, provide advice, even do ultrasounds or biopsies, would fit into the back of the RV. I also could predict that federal funding for reproductive health would be whittled down to nothing, and I knew that I did not want to rely on grants, donations, or government money. We were going to build this privately, and in the same manner as medical practices everywhere, we would bill insurance and build a business.

My friends and family, all more business-savvy than I am, had many questions to which I did not have answers—a clinic like the one I envisioned did not really exist. "Who is going to want to see their gynecologist inside of an RV?"

My mother didn't understand who would drive the thirty-one-foot clinic.

"I am going to drive it," I answered her question over the phone.

"You know how to drive an RV?" She was incredulous.

"Mom, I perform robotic hysterectomies. I deliver babies by emergency surgery in under two minutes. Do you think that is easier than driving a bus? I can figure out how to drive an RV."

I was happy she wasn't around to see me pull into a gas station for the first time. I screamed out loud to myself behind the steering wheel when I realized I had not adjusted for the wide turning radius. Within the first week of purchasing the rig I had crunch marks on the outside bumpers, scars from all the places I had come too close to a post or gas station curb. Fortunately, I had

Nicholas, the Spanish-speaking attendant at my now go-to station, to help guide me. I rolled down the window and he directed me to back up, then pull back in, laughing the whole time.

During those days, I was also busy recruiting friends. One would help me rip the bed out of the back and reconfigure the room to make space for an exam bed. My daughter and I would pick out Home Depot vinyl flooring and cut the squares to size. My dear friend Kate, a seamstress, would spend days with me measuring curtain lengths, taking trips to the fabric store, sewing and hanging curtains and valances, covering pillows and stools to soften up the interior and give it a cozy and professional feeling. We found ourselves upside down, our arms tiring from trying to hold up fabric while using an electric drill to screw rods into flaky RV ceilings.

Most important, I needed staff to help me run the clinic. I called my two former employees Laura and Terra, who had been in job flux since Covid, and asked them whether they wanted to join me in this endeavor—I needed a manager and a medical assistant. They had been with me through Mermaid Hair, they were family, and I believed we were the right three people to start this "just risky enough" adventure. They tell me now that after I called, they checked in with each other. "What does she mean by 'inside of an RV'? Is she kidding?" But they said yes anyway.

When I launched the mobile clinic, my father did not discuss it with me for two years. It seemed like the decade leading to the clinic had finally given him the gift he had always dreamt of for me—a private practice, a respected position at the hospital. I was a surgeon *and* an obstetrician *and* a mother *and* a wife. His

American Dream for me was complete. And now, it seemed, I was trading it in for thirty-one feet and four tires that would inevitably go flat on a secluded road.

"I built it as a fully functional doctor's office, Dad," I said to him over the phone, repeating answers to his initial concerns. "I can do everything in the RV that I did in my old clinic."

"You would attract five times as many patients if you opened up another office in a building. You would be busier than ever. You would be secure."

"I don't want to be in a building, Dad. That's the point. Buildings are in fixed locations. Buildings can't be nimble. Buildings don't meet people where they are. Buildings are the old way. . . ."

"You don't know who will show up to a mobile clinic," he insisted. "You might end up on the side of a road. You might get lost. Strange people might show up. You never know who or what will knock on the door. . . ."

This is where he had me, or I had him. "Keep talking, Dad." I laughed. "Now I'm getting excited."

The days inside the RV could not have proven him more wrong. It turns out that an aspirational idea attracts aspirational people. One by one, patients showed up. And when they did, Laura and Terra and I greeted them with hugs and gratitude from the front room of the clinic—seated on the brown vinyl couch, cozied together at the dining table booth. I asked every new patient how they heard about us and thanked each one for taking a chance on our unique model of care.

"I understand it might seem strange to see your gynecologist inside of an RV, so thank you," I still say to each one.

Some of the patients were as apprehensive as my father but showed up anyway. "I felt like I needed something different," some would say. "I just wanted to get in with someone quickly," others would confess. A few admitted that their loved ones were concerned when they learned that the doctor's office was in an RV, in a parking lot or down a country road.

Mom! Where r u? I can see your location. R u ok???!!! A new patient turned her phone screen to me as soon as she sat down. **I thought u said u had a doctor's appointment. Ur in the middle of nowhere! Horror face emoji. Crying emoji.**

"It's my fourteen-year-old daughter," my patient said, laughing. "She tracks me, and it looks like I am in the middle of an open field."

Mothers started bringing in their daughters—teenagers with heavy bleeding and pain, those who needed their first Pap smear in their early twenties. Daughters recommended their mothers—women who had not been to the doctor in over a decade, women who were sweating through their sheets at night due to menopause and zombie-walking through their days due to lack of sleep. Husbands, wives, boyfriends, girlfriends were great sources of discovery. Sometimes a pickup truck would pull up outside the clinic with the driver dropping off their loved one for a highly anticipated appointment. They were suffering from endometriosis and nobody would listen. They were scared to get pregnant and nervous about birth control. They were trying to get pregnant without success. They were hoping to start hormones for gender transition. They had not had a period in over a year. Partners searched for doctors online and discovered our alternative model of care. They read the reviews, and they convinced their wife, sister, roommate, friend to give us a chance. I imagined them booking an appointment, saying, "It's not like the traditional healthcare system has helped you to this point. Why not try something different?"

On a rainy February evening, with water pelting the RV sideways and the wipers on full speed, I sat behind the wheel. That night, we were on a mission. The usual plan for the clinic was to locate permanent spots to park each week, partner with community programs or medical offices, and plant us within neighborhoods where patients could schedule appointments and where our presence would become regular and known. It would be nearly impossible to drive the vehicle around for house calls and I knew we needed a way to see a dozen or more patients a day to keep us financially solvent. But a woman had reached out to us; she had been admitted at the hospital for three days after bleeding through her clothing and was found to be severely anemic. She was stabilized and then discharged. Nobody had diagnosed the reason behind her bleeding and because she was young, only in her twenties, serious causes for concern were dismissed. She was also Latina and considered overweight by medical standards, and after we talked to her, she felt that this may have contributed to medical bias and a dismissal of her symptoms. Could she be seen in our clinic? she asked. And could we come to her house? She worked all day and could not take more time off from work.

We had only been in business a few months and a house call in the clinic felt like a luxurious but appropriate adventure. I had not counted on the darkness and the slickness of the rain as I headed up the freeway, a thirty-minute drive to her home. But wasn't this the purpose of the clinic?

I turned off the freeway and pulled up next to the sidewalk in front of her home as planned.

"We just need to do a pregnancy test and then I can do the biopsy," I told her as she walked into the RV door.

"This is *cute*!" she exclaimed, and looked around. I looked with her. It *was* cute. I had not yet put up the twinkling fairy lights or refined the exam room with a proper table—that would come later. But on this blustery night, we were cozy inside. The generator hummed and the unit was warm. Laura had met me there in her own car and was prepping the area for an exam. Our patient had just gotten home from work and changed into her pajamas. We positioned her on the table; I inserted the speculum and did a biopsy of the tissue lining of her uterus.

"I'm sorry this wasn't done for you before," I said.

An endometrial biopsy is not a comfortable procedure, but our patient breathed through the steps of having a small pipette inserted through her cervix and into her uterus to suction a small amount of blood and tissue. The sample was placed in formalin and into the refrigerator to be sent to the lab the next day. After hugs and a goodbye, Laura and I packed up the way we had quickly become accustomed to. Trash bags tied off and ready to be disposed. Cabinets secured with bungee cords. The slides that expanded our space brought back in.

"See ya tomorrow," I called out to Laura as she stepped out toward her car.

A few days later Laura and I sat at our little clinic coffee table—a booth that most families would use to eat breakfast at a campsite. I scrolled through lab results, reviewing numbers and Pap smears that dropped into my chart.

Adenocarcinoma of the uterus. The words popped out of our patient's pathology report. I did a double take. *Adenocarcinoma?* In her twenties?

"Laura." I looked across the table. "Her biopsy came back. She has uterine cancer."

"Whoa," Laura replied. I reread the words and gazed out the window. We were inside a mobile home. From the outside, we could be anybody in Oregon, on a road trip to the coast, driving around the country. But instead, we had parked in front of a teacher's house, invited her inside at seven o'clock on a rainy night, performed an endometrial biopsy, and diagnosed her with cancer. Our little clinic had done this. Without the trappings of a large hospital system. Without all of the fuss. Our patient was referred to an oncologist and with conservative management, she was able to keep her uterus and still consider becoming pregnant one day, because her cancer was caught early. It felt like a turning point, and one early in the life of the clinic. We felt that if we could diagnose cancer in the back room, we could do anything.

Healthcare didn't have to be so complicated, I thought. Healthcare could be butcher paper rolled on the wall of a concrete hut in Bolivia, and the willingness to get behind the wheel.

I run the day-to-day operations of the mobile clinic like I parent my children—there are some set rules and expectations, but I stay open to the variations that are sure to insert themselves into our days. I often say that when I started the clinic I knew very well how to doctor and how to care for patients, but there was much I had to learn. Such as how to empty the gray and black sewage water, get propane for the generator, and troubleshoot the air-conditioning. I also had not anticipated the way the clinic would evolve as our community learned about us and shared their experiences. While I was there to serve the clinic, the clinic was there to provide what healthcare was often lacking—a space for inclusive LGBTQIA+ care, neurodivergent patients, patients with histories of medical trauma, and in general, anybody who had determined that the current medical system could be better, who recognized their providers were lacking in some way, either in accessibility, compassion, or availability. Somehow, within thirty-one feet, we became what I dubbed a "joyful fuck-you" to the medical system, and my patients represented an equally aspirational "be the change you want to see in the world" community.

When Kristy and Maggie arrived at their appointment the first time, they plopped onto the brown vinyl couch that served as our initial greeting area. They rushed in after work and giggled as they finished each other's sentences. Kristy shared how they had been married a few years and had spent $30,000 so far on fertility treatments. They were down to their final vial of donor sperm after already attempting six times; each vial cost them $1,300—no small price for a couple of milliliters of genetic gold.

"We can't afford to keep going to the fertility clinic and we have already spent our savings," Kristy said.

They had searched for other doctors in the area, stumbled upon the site for our mobile clinic, and decided we were worth giving a shot. I explained that while I didn't specialize in fertility, I had become interested in queer conception, especially as a matter of health equity; after all, most queer couples don't have true, pathologic infertility, they just require a more creative path for insemination. And many couples, like this one, did not have insurance plans that covered infertility, which could have a starting price tag in the tens of thousands.

"Well," I said, looking at the two young women on the couch, each of them with eyes that searched my face for reasons to hope. "I see two uteri, four fallopian tubes, and four ovaries in front of me. There's probably something we can do with that."

In the end I decided to treat them both with follicle-inducing hormones and bring them both in for ultrasounds, deciding which one to inseminate with the final vial based on the size and appearance of the eggs they formed in their ovaries. Ultimately Maggie, the partner whose body had not gone through as many of the fertility attempts, seemed to be the better candidate.

For many years I dreamt of a way to help couples conceive at home versus in a sterile office, legs in stirrups, staring at a ceiling LED light. Traditional medical setups are not conducive to house calls or in-home care, but being mobile allowed me this flexibility. When it came time for Maggie's intrauterine insemination, I offered to do it in their home, and they excitedly agreed.

Timing is everything when it comes to scheduled fertility, and so we arranged for me to bring the supplies I needed to their place after work on a Friday. The afternoon before we had confirmed one to two plump eggs in her ovary and administered a hormonal trigger shot to help push one out toward the fallopian tube. The goal would be to time the introduction of sperm through a tube into her uterus in a way that at least one sperm would meet one egg, and make the baby they had spent the past three years dreaming of.

At the end of our clinic day, Laura helped me gather the supplies I needed—gloves, a speculum, a small tube to draw up the semen and insert into the uterus, a clamp to grasp the cervix, and a tiny light. I placed them into a cardboard box and with a marking pen labeled it "Home IUI Kit," laughing at its simplicity. I messaged Kristy and Maggie on my way to give them time to remove the semen sample from the dry ice in which it was delivered. Kristy had it thawing inside of her bra, against her skin, when she let me in the door.

"Awww, look at this cute place." I marveled at the honor of being inside the home of my patients, a sacred element to the encounter I did not take for granted. The yard was meticulously planted with vegetables and flowers, which Kristy gave Maggie credit for. I greeted Maggie with a hug, and she reported that she felt well, albeit a bit bloated from the hormones.

We walked up the stairs to the bedroom where we had decided I could do the insemination. It felt only right to allow Maggie to lie comfortably in her own bed, and I knew as soon as the process was over, I could leave and allow them time as a couple to recover and rest together. From our small talk about their garden and the pets locked away in the extra bedroom, and some jokes about how we spent Friday nights in our pajamas, I could tell we were all a little nervous. This was the last vial of sperm, and the stakes were high; if this cycle did not work, they might not have the financial, physical, or emotional stamina to keep going.

Kristy helped Maggie prepare on the bed. I laid out my instruments and carefully drew up the sample into a sterile pipette. Without an exam table or stirrups, I simply took my seat on a low stool at the end of the bed, and Maggie scooted herself down toward the edge. When we realized she had nowhere to put her feet, I tapped the tops of my thighs and she rested them there while I inserted the speculum, and then the pipette. Within a minute we were done, and she was scooted back underneath the covers, Kristy bringing her water and asking what she wanted to order for Friday-night takeout.

As I had done just a few other times during my house calls, I collected my supplies, tucked the cardboard box underneath my arm, gave them each a hug goodbye, and snuck out the front door.

Seven weeks later in the back of the RV, using the ultrasound machine, we spotted two small gestational sacs with twin heartbeats. Sixteen weeks later we learned that Maggie was carrying their future children—not one but two healthy fetuses. When we recount the story of how these babies were made, they always remember the part when Maggie placed her feet on my thighs. Something so simple, something about humanity and a group of women working together to make what felt like the impossible possible.

Imperforate Patriarchy

2022

No matter where women are seen by their doctors, real life enters the exam room. There is no uterus that is not attached to its body, and no body that does not live in relationship with others—partners, parents, society. It is why the practice of medicine is often better than any TV drama. People walk in and their histories walk beside them, behind them, inside of them.

On one regular clinic day, I perched on my stool, close to the ground, facing the couch in order to be eye to eye with my patient. A mother was seated next to her fifteen-year-old daughter. Like many of the mobile clinic patients, they had found us through a Google search and were relieved to be greeted by Laura at the door, speaking Spanish, ushering them inside, and locking the door behind them.

"She's having a lot of belly pain." The mother did most of the talking, as expected with these young teenager appointments. Her daughter actually looked physically uncomfortable, one hand on her lower abdomen and nodding her head.

I asked the usual questions. When did the pain begin? Did it come and go? Were there any other symptoms? Nausea, vomiting, fevers? When did she start her period and was her pain worse with her cycles?

"She has not had a period yet," her mom replied, and her daughter nodded again. "We were wondering about that too."

The discussion led to an exam, and after I received permission from the patient to help her into stirrups and gently look inside, it was obvious to me. She had a condition known as an "imperforate hymen." Most women have a thin sheet of tissue covering their vaginal opening until it is disrupted—by exercise, riding a bike, tampons, or sexual activity. But even before this there is usually an opening in the sheet that allows blood to exit every month once periods start.

"There is no opening in this hymen—it is called an imperforate hymen," I explained to the teenager and her mother. We were seated back on the couch, the patient now dressed. I used a small whiteboard to draw what I meant. "I think you are in pain because there is no place for blood to exit. Your uterus is full of blood that can't escape. Who knows how long it has been collecting—maybe all year."

We confirmed this the next day with an ultrasound. The size of her uterus was that of a six-month pregnancy, but instead of a fetus filling the space, there was blood. It was no wonder she was in pain. Several liters of menstrual blood had stretched her uterus to her belly button.

I called the patient and her mother to describe to them the simple solution. I would take her to the operating room and cut a small hole into the hymenal sheet. This would allow the blood to exit and I would use a suction device to remove it all. Once the procedure was complete, she would feel a great relief and should also begin to have regular monthly periods. I could get her in the next day and put her out of this misery in twenty minutes.

Her mother asked whether she could call me back, and an hour later my phone rang. "Her father does not want her to have the surgery," she said. "He does not believe it will be a good idea. One day, when she wants to be married . . ." It took me a second to understand, but I got it—"breaking the hymen." This was how her traditional father had interpreted the surgery. What man would want to marry a woman with a "broken hymen"? How would she explain herself?

I felt my throat tighten. It was 2022 in America. I understood that in some countries women might be subjected to obtaining a "virginity certificate" prior to being married. I was aware that some brides-to-be were scared that if they did not bleed during their first time having intercourse with their husband, they would be accused of not being a virgin. And in certain cultures, and religions, not being a virgin has led to serious consequences, including public torture and death.

Study after study has disproved the theories of "virginity detection"—an actual hymen anatomically presents itself in many forms, just like every other part of our anatomy. Some hymens tear early in life; others have a stretchy quality. Others can remain partially intact, even in women who have been sexually active for years. I tell patients there is no such thing as a "virginity test," and anybody who claims to know of one has not spent as many years in between as many legs as a gynecologist.

"Would it be possible to speak with your husband?" I asked. I had not formulated what to say, but recalling the image of the teenager with her hand on her belly, her abdomen full of blood, I had to paint some sort of a picture for him to understand.

She called out to him, and I overheard their exchange in Spanish. From her instructive tone it was pretty clear that she was in fact the boss in the family; finally, he spoke into the phone. "Hola?"

We went back and forth for several minutes, as I explained the medical condition and he haltingly described his worry. It was not just about her, I was finally able to ascertain. It was not just about his control. What if, he said after a pause, what if her future husband not only rejected her but caused her to be rejected and humiliated by everyone around her? What would that do to her? he asked.

My stance softened. I had assumed he, the father, the man, held a patriarchal choke hold on his daughter. In fact, I was surprised to realize he also felt the choke hold on himself, in having a daughter who might be subjected to outdated machismo, misogynist ideals. One day, when she was no longer his responsibility, would she be cast out, shamed, or even physically hurt?

How many times had I heard different variations of this fear played out over the years? Pregnant teenagers forced to end their pregnancies by their parents, others hidden, their newborns secretly given away. I also encountered victims of female genital mutilation whose mothers had held them down as children, allowing the violent removal of their external genitalia in the context of preserving cultural norms and myths. In those instances, parents, including mothers, supported the practice to control a girl's sexuality or to ensure her "purity" and fidelity for marriage; the consequences of not doing so felt to them much worse. Those patients ended up in my clinic decades later with multiple chronic conditions—pain, inability to complete penetrative sex in order to achieve pregnancy, lack of sensation, PTSD, and on and on. Even the simpler act of attempting to ban birth control, or fomenting fear about the use of contraception, was a mechanism of controlling sexuality in our own country.

The father and I continued talking. I kept bringing it back to his daughter, her pain, the inevitability of needing to create some normalcy in her anatomy, the actual fact that we had no other option—what was the alternative here? He became attuned to her suffering, and in the end, he relented. There would continue to be fear and discussion, I was sure. I could imagine that his own sense of power felt challenged and that he would require a reconciliation with the reality of raising a daughter, an eventual sexual being who would be out in the world. But in that moment, he put his wife back on the line and we moved forward with scheduling the surgery. Less than twenty-four hours later, our patient woke up from anesthesia, smiling. She was no longer in pain, and I got to witness her father standing next to her, holding her hand, when she opened her eyes.

Navigating a father's role in the decision-making for a teenage girl's reproductive health felt like a throwback that would take me back to Mehry. When women from asylum-seeking countries would show up at the door of my clinic, or the hospital, from Afghanistan, Sudan, Ethiopia, Yemen, their hair covered with scarves, their children as interpreters, Mehry would appear by their side. She is me, I heard her say once, and then again. She is almost you, was the implication.

When she returned to the hammam the following week, Mehry learned that it was the aunties all along. They were the ones with the special herbal tea. They were the ones who knew just the right tincture of dried pomegranate, saffron, mugwort, and rue. There were likely other elements mixed in, but these were the ones Nilufar listed. This time, when Mehry walked by, the aunties clicked their tongues and gave her what appeared to be supportive nods.

"Too many babies and a woman's heart will grow too large. One day, she will be birthing her eleventh, her twelfth baby. The next day, dead. The muscle of her heart too tired, too weak to go on." Number one leaned in toward Mehry and whispered in a loud hiss. Mehry could smell her breath, the stench of mint leaves and stale feta cheese from her breakfast.

"Yes, without an end to it, you will be fifty years old having babies. And then what? Your babies will be having their babies. No end to the babies." Number two said it to her back as Mehry quickly passed them by, hoping Nilu would be waiting for her in the changing area.

She had no intention of bathing that day. That day was a business trip to the bathhouse. Instead of toting her usual change of clothing and toiletries, Mehry had emptied her bag to make room for whatever it was that Nilufar was bringing.

"Mehry!" Nilu spotted her from across the pool and called her name. She motioned for her to step into one of the private changing areas.

“I told the attendant I was on my period and would not be bathing today,” Nilu confided. “So, she will leave us alone.” Nilu was more flushed than usual, and it occurred to Mehry that this was a big deal to her too.

“It is very simple,” Nilu said as she pulled a brown paper sack out of her purse, opening it briefly for Mehry to peer in and smell the contents inside. It looked similar to the Darjeeling tea she drank several times a day. But the smell was more pungent and caused a momentary sting inside her nose.

Step by step Nilu walked her through the process. How many tablespoons. How long to steep. To be prepared for the nasty taste. To sweeten with dates. To start over again the next day should she vomit within an hour. To expect abdominal cramps. Terrible pains. Pains that would cause her to double over and spend hours on the toilet. But not to be afraid of the pain—that just meant it was working. And then to be prepared for the bleeding. A lot of bleeding. Passing gobs of blood and tissue. Pomegranate-sized clots. Allow it all to pass; don’t try to stop the passage. Monitor her heart rate with her fingers to her wrist. Drink a lot of water in the process. And if she felt dizzy or like fainting, go to the hospital. Tell her husband she was having an abnormal period. Too much bleeding. Make sure to see a doctor. Or midwife. Do not mention the tea. Never mention the tea. This is a bad period. Or, perhaps, a spontaneous miscarriage. One or the other. Both common and acceptable excuses for hemorrhage.

Mehry listened closely. She thought about writing down notes but changed her mind. She did not want any evidence of this conversation. She was meeting Nilufar and receiving a gift of tea. Nothing more. She understood. Nilu had done this before—more than once before and everything had been okay. She would be okay too.

"One more thing, Mehry *jan*." Nilu lowered her voice, surprisingly low.

"It is about *Ruh*, you know, ensoulment. The moment when the growing fetus gets its soul." Her words were slow and measured. Mehry understood. This was not about judgment but Islamic law.

"Ensoulment begins at a hundred and twenty days. You understand that, right, Mehry *jan*? Whatever you decide to do, do before a hundred and twenty days."

"*Baleh azizam*, yes, my dear," Mehry said while lowering her eyes to the ground. This is where the practical became personal. Mentioning the soul. She would leave the calculations for when she returned home. How many days into the pregnancy she was, and when she would hit the 120-day mark.

"I have to go," Nilu said as she folded the top of the bag tightly and pushed it into Mehry's arms. "God willing, this will be over soon." She kissed each of Mehry's cheeks and stepped quickly out of the room.

"*Inshallah*, God willing," Mehry replied. She stuffed the paper bag into her purse, fanned her flushed cheeks with her hand, and walked, head tall, back straight, out of the bathhouse.

Betrayal

2022

The birth of the mobile clinic brought with it small victories and a return to the joyful, independent practice of medicine. But in 2022 there was an undercurrent of change happening on every level—national strategies to reduce access to reproductive care were leading headlines, anti-transgender activism was becoming more visible, and whether we would have a future that afforded us the same bodily autonomy we were accustomed to had become part of the daily discourse. I questioned how to market our clinic, whether to put our name and branding on the outside or to remain incognito. It felt like a dilemma I would not have considered a decade before. I debated with my closest trusted advisors how to exist in an increasingly hostile world—could we remain unmarked on the side of the road? What person would trust a doctor's office that was not only in an RV but didn't even have a name on the door?

Despite the uncertainty, we continued to grow our services and patients continued to show up. The RV offered everything I could offer as an ob-gyn—annual exams with Pap smears, treatment for chronic conditions such as endometriosis and PCOS (polycystic ovary syndrome), menopause management, gender-affirming care with hormone replacement, placing IUDs and Nexplanon rods, and the occasional diagnosing of cancer—cervical tumors, ovarian masses, uterine bleeding. I also integrated early pregnancy appointments into our schedule, with an ultrasound machine in the back, and provided first-trimester pregnancy care as we are medically trained to do: establish whether a pregnancy is in the right place and growing, evaluate the mother's medical condition, offer counseling and guidance, determine from the patient whether the pregnancy is desired, and if not, counsel about options, giving every patient the ability to decide what would be best for them, including resources for adoption and abortion.

At the same time, my marriage was beginning to break down—the synchronicity we had as co-parents when the kids were young changed as they grew older, and it was as if we had become the near strangers we were when we got married. To take breaks from the tension, I occasionally flew home with the kids to California to see my parents. There was also a growing strain with my father. While we interacted politely, I was aware that he did not approve of the clinic, and now with a potential divorce on the horizon, the tenuousness of my life seemed at an all-time high. I understood; there was an instability to what I was doing that was at odds with the traditional doctor life. The clinic was not making me enough to live on, and I worked extra-hard twenty-four-hour shifts at the hospital to subsidize my income. I would soon be out of the house we had built, and my future was no longer predetermined.

When we arrived on a Friday afternoon, the living room basement was how it always was—crowded, loud, warm with food and sunshine streaming through the windows. Like so many kids of immigrants, I grew up in a home where the front door was always open and in entered cousins, uncles, family friends no matter the time of day or night. I loved the bustle of it, with everyone effortlessly toggling between English and Farsi. My mother zipped around, plating food and clearing dishes, smiling and chatting with my children. My dad held court in his recliner, engaged in conversation with a dear family friend, someone I had known since childhood. We had chatted a bit when I arrived, but it wasn't until later in the night, when all the extras had left, when my daughter tucked into a bedroom to watch TV and my son snuggled next to my dad on the opposite couch, assisting with an online poker game, that the friend—we'll call him Darren—started talking to me.

"You've heard what they are doing at Planned Parenthood, right?" He was pacing around behind the love seat I sat on. That was one thing about Darren: I never seemed to get him in still conversation or with good eye contact. There was another thing about Darren I had learned over the years: Don't talk politics around him. Or conspiracy theories. Or the president. Any president. He had recently retired, and it was clear to us that he was spending more and more time in the darkest corners of the internet and consuming news bites 24-7.

"Ummm." I looked toward my parents, a subtle Mayday attempt. My mom did not seem to notice that Darren was still there—she was busy next to the sink in the corner, washing dishes and putting fruit slices onto a platter.

"I'm not sure what you're referring to," I said nervously. Don't engage, I told myself. I looked over at my father on the opposite couch to see whether he was listening and might give me an out. He and my son laughed and tapped the keyboard—two pair! they announced in unison.

"You haven't heard about how they are conducting ceremonies?" Darren stopped walking and stood face-to-face with me now. Except that he was hovering above me. His eyes were dark and his eyebrows tight, thick with flecks of gray.

"What kind of ceremonies?" I kept my voice neutral. Here it goes, I thought. Deep breaths, no response. You can get through this, I coached myself.

"Where they cut the babies out of the mothers at like thirty-seven weeks. They cut them out and kill them and then hold ceremonies where they light candles around the dead babies."

Heart pounding. Body sweating. Face heating. I felt it all in my physiology, the absurdity of what he was saying to me. To *me*, of all people. Did he not know what I did for a living?

"Listen, Darren," I started. "I am not sure where you are getting this information, but . . ." It was the last little bit of calm I had left in my voice and body.

"This information is everywhere. I can show you the videos. The videos are out there. Do you want me to show you the videos?" His voice was raised now.

"Look," I said, matching his volume. "Now you are crossing a line that I can't pretend is okay." I turned my body to face him completely. "You are talking about my profession, my expertise, my career. I know what an abortion is; I have performed abortions. And I know the difference between an abortion and what you are talking about. I spend every day of my life making sure that pregnant women and their babies are safe, I stay up all night monitoring heart rates to make sure babies don't die, and you are trying to convince me that what you are talking about is true?!"

I had barely finished my sentence when his face, arms, and upper body were practically on top of me. Not touching me but close.

"You have performed abortions?! *You are disgusting*," he yelled. "*Disgusting, disgusting, disgusting!*" His finger was practically poking out my eyeball, his cheeks were red, and his entire figure menaced above me. "*I can't believe what you do. Disgusting!*"

I held my face still. His words seemed to fill the room, and I was certain somebody would intervene. I could feel my eyes stinging with tears, but I clenched my jaw, breathed through my nose, and froze. "*Disgusting. Disgusting.*" He repeated the words again and again. I was afraid to move. If I moved, would I make myself vulnerable? A predator pounces when it's threatened, right? Play dead, play dead, play dead. My body stayed motionless, my chest barely rising.

My years of training filled my mind in those moments when the big face was screaming into mine. All the early-morning awakenings, the long labors, the holding of hands of parents who had lost their babies, the celebrations of births in the C-section room. I remembered training as a medical student in the Bronx, greeting young women who had boarded buses and traveled for days to escape their abusers, their rapists, seeking abortions in the first or second trimester of their pregnancies, before legal limits expired. Their stories lived with me—the future seekers, the ones who escaped. I worked with colleagues who stayed up night after night making sure premature babies survived, and others who spent a decade studying fetal anomalies and how to create better lives for these children. I performed abortions as part of the scope of physical and emotional health for women, for reproductive justice, the right to bodily autonomy, self-determination. But now this? This person? Who had never stepped foot inside of an ob-gyn office. Who knew nothing of pregnancy complications or sepsis from early rupture of amniotic fluid membranes or genetic abnormalities. Who had never sat with a woman who grieved the loss of her child or the loss of her childhood. He stood over me with a pointed finger and claimed to know what I was. "*Disgusting*." The word came out of him again.

"Enough!" I yelled back at him. "Get out of my face." I stood up. That got my parents' attention. My father looked up. My mother slowly started walking toward us. "I have to leave, I am getting out of here." I was crying then and reaching for my car keys. It was midnight and nobody seemed to understand what had happened.

"Don't go, Mary," my mother called after me. "Where are you going?"

I drove down the driveway with no idea where I was actually going. I drove around my small hometown for an hour, put gas in the car, drove a little bit more. I was shaking and crying and confused. What had just happened? I repeated to myself out loud in the car over and over. What the hell was that?

When I returned Darren was gone. My children were asleep, and my parents were sitting on the couch waiting for me. I could barely look at them.

"What happened, Mary?" they asked.

"What happened? What happened? You were both here. Did you not hear what he said? Did you not hear what he called me over and over again?"

"I wasn't paying attention," my mother responded. "I don't know why you would talk to him about those things anyway."

"You shouldn't talk politics with him," my dad suggested.

I stared at the two of them, trying to digest what they'd said. This was a feeling too familiar—something about my convictions had put me on the outside. I turned and walked into the guest bedroom, shut the door, and locked it. I had never locked myself inside a bedroom before, especially not at my own parents' house, but I felt afraid. Who knew what Darren might be capable of given that reaction, given what he believed? I lay in bed but didn't fall asleep. Was this the turning point? Was this where hypervigilance became the new normal?

I left the house early the next morning, crossed the Bay Bridge, and spent the day hiking the hills in foggy San Francisco. I climbed Coit Tower, which was not visible from the road. I felt safer in the fog, where I could not be seen. Sitting on a boulder, wrapping my light coat around me, I felt Mehry's hand slip into mine. She squeezed for a moment. Come, she said. I have something to show you.

The brown paper sack sat in a small wooden cabinet above her bed. Mehry could not risk anybody finding it. She was sixty-seven days into the pregnancy. This was according to the last time she slept with her husband. Eighty-one days since her last period. She had not asked Nilu which number to use. The day she knew the baby was conceived or the last day she bled? To be safe, she decided to go with the larger number. Eighty-one. That left her about five weeks. She marked a date in her pocketbook calendar. An *X* in the box. *Ruh*. Ensoulment. The moment the multiplying tadpole cells receive their future human form.

Mehry was not a scholar of Islam. She could barely consider herself Muslim for how little she knew of the Qur'an. She simply could not keep her attention on matters of religion. Fortunately, her husband was also quite loose in his interpretation of the Holy Book and did not require her to abide in any strict way.

But *Ruh* was a different matter—not entirely the word of the Qur'an but an interpretation of the words of the Prophet. She had always listened when it came to the subject of ensoulment, described to her, by her grandmother, as the breath of an angel. That day, returning home with the brown sack, she entered her husband's office knowing he was away for several days again. It smelled of cigar and paper. Meticulously clean with shelves that spanned across the entire wall. His massive desk sat in the middle of the room. On it, a stand for one of his most treasured pens. Montblanc, she thought to herself. The only pen he would ever use.

Mehry rarely entered the office and had little interest in staying. This was her husband's sanctuary, made for a man who spent most of his days in the world, dealing in business, negotiating with men from the lowest levels of land maintenance to the highest level of government. This space—dark, quiet, and warm—belonged to him.

She moved quickly toward the bookshelf and scanned the titles.

She was not the fastest reader but knew what she was looking for. She had heard the name many times in her childhood: Book of Hadith. It was an interpretation of the sayings of the Prophet Mohammed. There were several books with similar names. Pulling out the first one, she scanned until she came to the section she was looking for: *Ruh*. What did it say about *Ruh*?

> Every one of you is collected in the womb of his mother for the first forty days,
>
> then he becomes a clot for another forty days, and then a piece of flesh for another forty days.
>
> Then Allah sends an angel to breathe the soul into his body.

That night, late, after her husband had retreated to his bedroom, after the kids were long asleep, Mehry boiled the water. She could not risk getting any closer to the *Ruh*. What if she had miscalculated and the *Ruh* was to arrive the next day? What if, worse yet, it had already landed?

Mehry picked out a separate mug for the poison tea. She did not want to look at the color of the drink and could not imagine it sitting in one of her delicate glasses. Her eyes were wide-open as she unrolled the top of the paper sack and measured three scoops of the strong-smelling herbs into the bottom of an old teapot she had dug out while cleaning the kitchen. Not the dainty one with the rose on the side.

She understood deep in her core the purpose of this brewing and steeping, and, eventually, the drinking. This was a death. Perhaps the baby was not a baby yet. Perhaps there was no soul. But every day Mehry watched her children with an awareness of what she would be losing. And also gaining. Losing the soul of the baby. Perhaps regaining hers, which had been lost.

The teapot filled with hot water. Leaves from the herbs both sank to the bottom and floated to the top. Mehry gave the water a few stirs with a spoon and then waited, much past the time that Nilu had suggested. But Mehry felt that it was right. Why not make sure it was as strong as it needed to be?

For fifteen minutes she sat with her hands crossed on her lap and rocked herself. She had chosen a poem to repeat while she drank the drink and began to murmur the words to herself.

For God to make love,
For the divine alchemy to work,
The Pitcher needs a still cup.

She had asked her Book of Hafiz for the poem to recite at this moment. It was a practice passed down by her grandmother, and then her mother. Hold the book in your hand and ask it a question. And then open to the page that will recite your answer.

Why ask Hafiz to say
Anything more about
Your most vital requirement?

When she had opened to the poem of "A Still Cup," she gasped as she always did with Hafiz. How did the book know? How did Hafiz seem to always have the words to match? This was a moment of divine alchemy.

She said the words as she poured the tar-colored liquid into the mug and brought it to her lips. She had decided not to add the dates. No sweetness in this moment. She would taste the bitter. She would swallow without a gag or holding her nose.

In one minute, it was over. The drink was gone, within her. She felt a heave, a rising within, but she told herself she could only do this one time. If she vomited, it would be over. She was not doing this again the next day. That alone kept the drink down. She disposed of the brine and sludge at the bottom of the pot, scraped them back into the brown sack, and stuffed them together into the bottom of the wastebasket.

"Poison!" she whispered as she shoved the remains of the liquid down the sink and rinsed the mug before also adding it to the waste can.

"The pitcher needs a still cup," she repeated. Trembling with what she had just done, sweat coating the inside of her nightdress, she made her way to the bedroom. She did not bother to remove her robe or slippers, crawled under the covers, and wept until she fell asleep.

When I returned to my parents' house for one final day and night, I barely spoke and locked the bedroom door. I called Keith to tell him I needed a few days to myself and that when the kids and I returned, I would be leaving by myself on a road trip. He didn't ask any questions, helped me pack my car, and stood in the driveway with the kids, waving goodbye.

Stanley, Idaho

2022

When I was sixteen years old my father took me and my younger brothers on a two-week summer road trip. I don't know whether my dad enjoyed anything more than unplanned, unscheduled time touring the country. He loved living in America—a place that offered kids' meals with toys for $3.99 on the way to some of the most breathtaking scenery in the world. Plunging water-laced canyons. Rocky fortresses heated by sun-fire. Trees with trunks wide enough for the station wagon to pass through. Ocean waves taller than a house. We somehow drove south through the Mojave Desert, passing Las Vegas, and also managed to visit Sun Valley and then Stanley, Idaho. My father, for all of his "tunnel vision" talk during the school year, transformed into an excited young boy on vacation. He threw us into drive-by motel swimming pools fully clothed to cool us down when the air conditioner of the car stopped working. He sweet-talked our way into fancy resort hot tubs even though we were staying at the less expensive place down the street. On hikes he jumped into waterfalls, whooping and making us think he would drown due to hypothermia. And in Stanley, he pulled into a fish farm, paid ten dollars per child, and gave us the gift of catching dozens of fish that we proudly reeled in and held up for photos.

We only spent one afternoon in Stanley—there was barely anything there. I remembered some ice cream after the fishing and then moving on to the next town to sleep. But I also remembered standing on an open road, staring at a wildflower meadow full of buffalo, framed by the Sawtooth Mountains. And I remembered thinking: I will be back here one day.

The day after we returned from California, my nervous system rattled, I packed a duffel bag and my paddleboard, kissed my children goodbye, and embarked on the nine-hour drive to Stanley. I booked a small room on the outskirts of town and spent the drive in clichéd solo road trip mode—blasting music and singing, crying to passages out of my audiobook, confiding in my best friend, then repeating it all over again. I pulled into Stanley just before dark, and when I smelled the trees, saw the stars and the shadow of the mountains, I knew I had come back to the right place.

My research before going to sleep prepped me for the next day. I would swing by the one bakery in town to grab a coffee, then make my way to the Salmon River just a mile down the road. I had read about a spot where the hot springs water entered the river just below the road and knew that was where I wanted to spend my morning.

I quickly discovered that this was a not-so-secret destination for many young tech nomads who learned that they could travel and work in the most beautiful places around the country. There were quite a few Sprinter vans parked along the road. A couple greeted me as I climbed down the rocks, a towel in one hand, my latte balanced in my other. They were taking photos of hemp-based products on rocks next to the water. The beautiful woman of the couple posed with the bottles in her bikini. Her boyfriend, the photographer, snapped pictures. "We work for this company. Our job is to travel to places where we can take aesthetic photographs of the products in nature," they explained.

I thought about my residency hours, the overnights at the hospital, the hemorrhages, Darren's tirade. "I think I picked the wrong career," I told them, perched in my own private pool of hot water created by the river rocks.

Couples came and went and I stayed. The early morning turned to midmorning and then it was close to noon. I realized the motion of the river pushed cold water in and out of the natural pools, and I made a pastime of moving my rocks around to get the perfect temperature. Just as I found perfection, a rush of hot water would make it too hot, or a crack in the rock wall would bring in cooler water. It was a meditation, a perfect distraction, to spend the morning in the pools, chatting with other people as they came and created their own little oases, stayed a while, then left. I didn't want to ever leave. I could stay in the rocks and the warm and the cool, the sound of the river, the leaves overhead, forever. I could put it all behind me—the clinic, the stress, the politics, the people. I would invite my kids to join me—they would love this beaver life. But everyone else, they could stay where they were. This was an exclusive sanctuary.

I was lost in these thoughts, and the pools had been empty for a while, when I heard the sound of two women's voices coming from the path. The friends were sliding, hanging on to each other, and laughing as they made their way down to the river.

"Hellooo!" they called out to me. "How's the water?"

"Perfect!" I yelled back. "Come on in!"

They were older than me, in their seventies, I guessed, as they approached the rocky pool next to me and started stripping down to their swimsuits. One carried a small cooler that she opened to start to make drinks. "Gin and tonics!" she declared.

"I'm a raisin," I confessed to them. "I've been in here for hours. I don't want to leave."

"Don't leave." The one working the bar started mixing ice cubes with a shot of gin. "We just got here!"

I learned that they had been travel companions for more than a decade, one married, one single, and every year they planned trips together despite living in separate states. They had just arrived in Stanley but had been here before, many times before. And it was clear that their primary purpose was to spend time with each other, tell stories, and have a good laugh.

"We both worked in the medical field, and we are now both retired," they shared with me.

Of course they were. I was in my own version of heaven and these two were the ghosts of my Christmas future.

"So do I have this to look forward to?" I asked, motioning at the two of them, their feet in the hot pool, sipping their drinks. "Because, I'm not going to lie, it hasn't been that easy lately."

"Listen." Woman number one leaned in, her glass in her hand. "It is never easy. It is never going to be easy. So, what do we do?" She leaned back onto the rock she was propped on.

"I don't know," I said. "What do you do?"

"This!" She clinked glasses with her friend. "We just keep on going. And we turn to the people we can turn to. Here. You need a drink."

With that, she cleaned out my paper coffee cup and mixed me a gin and tonic. I moved out of the hot pool and sat on a rock in the river, and from our respective perches we talked and told stories and shared tales from our work and our lives. When it was finally time for me to make my way back up to my car, they said to me, "We need to take a picture of you right now. For you to look back on. What a perfect scene. But take one of our glasses; can't have a paper coffee cup instead of a real gin and tonic glass."

I handed them my phone and posed back on the rock. They snapped a photo of me wearing a big sweatshirt and an even bigger grin. I stared at it back in my car. I didn't look like I was wearing bottoms. But I looked as happy as I had ever been. It's my most favorite picture of me, I thought—this bottomless, sun-kissed, smiling me. I glanced one more time at their figures in the rocks, chatting away, before I pulled a U-turn and drove away.

My last morning in Idaho was June 24, 2022. I woke up in my cell service–free cabin and luxuriated in my blissfully serene final few hours off the grid. Eventually, I got in my car and headed home.

The pinging began as soon as I approached the town center. A bazillion text messages from everyone who knew and loved me.

The Supreme Court had done it, and our country woke up to a new reality under the *Dobbs* decision. "I can't believe it." Crying face emoji, sobbing face emoji, angry face emoji, skull and crossbones.

The *Dobbs* decision that day overturned the constitutional right to abortion established by *Roe v. Wade* and *Planned Parenthood v. Casey*. This decision returned the authority to regulate abortion to individual states, which state by state had already begun dismantling abortion rights. The significance of *Dobbs* was that it would not only affect women in states that overturned abortion but decrease access to all types of reproductive healthcare, close clinics, drive doctors out of those areas, and possibly set a precedent for a nationwide abortion ban and all the consequences of reduced access to care.

I picked up a large coffee from the Stanley Baking Company and started the nine-hour drive back to Portland. I wish I had thought to time-lapse video-record the drive because, in my somewhat numb, somewhat agitated state of mind, I did recognize the irony of my road trip. It was the distance the women of Idaho would now have to travel to obtain an abortion, since Idaho had enacted one of the strictest antiabortion laws in the country.

"How is anybody surprised?" I said out loud again and again.

Arriving back in Portland that day in June, I felt the stillness. When I walked into my usual coffee shop the next morning, the barista looked up at me, her eyes puffed and red from crying. I nodded, she nodded back, and I took my drink and stood next to her at the counter.

"What the fuck?" She shook her head. She was twenty-one years old, and her reproductive years were still ahead of her. I was forty-eight years old, and my fears of unintended pregnancy were basically behind me. This news was her news, but also mine. She was a person who could get pregnant and not have options around the pregnancy. I was a person whom politicians were vocally trying to criminalize. We were now in lockstep, handcuffed by our government's decision.

A year and a half earlier I had decided to start the mobile clinic. The idea had been brewing since 2016. One day, while I was seeing patients in my private practice, a pharmaceutical rep for IUDs and birth control pills stopped into the office to chat and fill our cabinets with free samples. I stood and looked at the rows of contraception and marveled that we took it all for granted. I had visited countries where birth control was banned. I'd worked in hospitals where sterilization and abortion were restricted. My parents left their home country as it transformed from a free democracy to a religious regime just forty years prior. Anything could happen in my lifetime; I felt it within me like muscle memory.

"What's going to happen when half the states ban abortion?" I repeated to anyone who would listen. "Where are those women going to go? Do you realize the doctors will also leave those states?!" In my idealistic mind, our mobile clinics would line borders, generous doctors and nurse practitioners working inside, greeting folks as they crossed from Eastern Idaho into Western Oregon.

"We've got you," we would say. In our vehicles, we could do what was needed—insert IUDs, offer annual wellness exams, biopsy abnormal lesions, prescribe hormones, and perform abortions. In the case of protest or threat or violence, I would hop behind the wheel, and we would peel out and move on to another safe and secret location. There would be a network of us, these reproductive health vans, and through encrypted messaging and walkie-talkies, we would communicate who needed what and where. The map in my mind showed us speckled across the country, one text away from providing care.

Then, just days after *Dobbs* was announced, news reports began to surface: *"They are going to arrest doctors for performing procedures, including, potentially, surgeries like ectopic pregnancies."*

"Insurance companies won't cover an abortion if someone goes out of a state."

"You might get arrested for doing an abortion on a woman from Idaho within Oregon."

"Report your doctor if you suspect criminal activity."

Anything could happen in my lifetime.

Part Three

Gas Gangrene

2023

Feeling the aftershocks of the *Dobbs* decision shifting the ground underneath, I return to work shifts at various hospitals in Oregon on the days I don't run the mobile clinic to subsidize my income and maintain my obstetric and surgical skills. It is noontime on a Friday at the hospital, and I am seated at a computer finishing up paperwork.

"What are you doing in twenty minutes?" Rebecca, one of the younger doctors, taps my knee.

I look up from my keyboard. I have just a few minutes before the patients start arriving again. I might take a bite of my salad while I follow up on lab results, finish chart notes, and call home to check on my family.

"Nothing important," I answer. "What's up?"

Rebecca pauses for just a second before answering, and it is in that moment of hesitancy that I sense urgency. She is the newest doctor in our group, just six months out of her training.

"What's going on?" I ask again.

I stand up so we are at eye level. We wear the matching hospital scrubs emblematic of our profession, but our personalities still peek through. A tiny sparkle emanates from the miniature stud in her nose. A silver clip holds back my bangs. We are grown-up girls. We are accomplished women. We are partners in our work. And she clearly needs to talk.

"I have a young woman who is septic. Pancytopenic. She has acute peritonitis. I need an assistant for the surgery." Her words flow quickly.

I am proficient in English, Farsi, and Spanish, but the most efficient language I speak is Doctor. Beginning in medical school, and then through immersion in our residencies, we adopt the tongue of those before us and indoctrinate those who come after us with the fluency of pseudonyms and abbreviations. Those few words of hers are all I need to hear.

"Let me know when you guys are wheeling back to the operating room," I tell her. "I'll head up."

"Okay," she says. "Thank you."

A few minutes later I run up the stairwell to meet Rebecca on the surgical floor. I am curious to learn more. Her initial description of this case was enough for me to postpone anything nonurgent this afternoon; now I need details.

"She's only twenty-six years old," Rebecca says in a low voice, our heads nearly touching underneath blue surgical bonnets. Despite her young age and petite frame, she assumes the air of surgeon, on this floor, in this outfit. She still appears calm, although an urgency cuts through the cadence of her words.

"She had an abortion at a clinic two days ago. It was her first pregnancy, unplanned. The guy really isn't in the picture," she continues.

We are the same height and similar builds and likely look like blue Thing 1 and Thing 2 whispering in the corner. We stand outside the doors of the OR while the team prepares the bed, counts instruments, and adjusts lights. In that moment, a stretcher is wheeled down the hall. The young woman is covered with a blanket, but she is shivering, and her face is pale. She produces a nervous smile when she sees Rebecca.

"We'll be right in!" Rebecca calls after her as she's wheeled into the operating room. We wait a moment for the doors to shut, then Rebecca turns back toward me.

"So, she became really sick. She went to the emergency room and then to her own doctor. He called me and I had her come to the hospital last night. Fever. Tons of belly pain. Her blood work is going the wrong direction even after antibiotics. She is septic and I am not totally sure what's wrong. I did a suction procedure last night to make sure nothing was left in the uterus. I got a CAT scan and now I'm really worried."

Rebecca pauses for a moment. She looks at me directly, her blue eyes a few inches from my face and steady.

"I think she might have gas gangrene."

I hear her say it and the hair on my arms spike. Gas gangrene. My lips, covered by a surgical mask, go dry. As far as medical terms go, to my mind gas gangrene is the most insidious. Beyond cancer. Beyond cardiac arrest. It is a term that evokes images nobody wants. Wounded soldiers on battlefields. Amputated limbs. Noxious fumes. Gas gangrene. It conjures another century, less advanced medicine, poor public health. Gas gangrene. In a game of word association, if you were to say "gas gangrene," I'd say back-alley abortion. Coat hanger. Blackened feet. Dead body.

I stand leaning against a large metal sink a few feet from the operating room doors. Rebecca has walked into the room to instruct the team. I take a minute to process.

Gas gangrene is so rare that its diagnosis is one of clinical suspicion and a process of elimination. A healthy vagina is rich with bacterial flora, a symphony of lactobacillus, streptococcus, and even *Clostridium perfringens.* They function together to do the job of well-advertised douches and vaginal cleanses. Maintain pH balance. Eat away the bad bugs, sustain the good.

But circumstances such as illness, pregnancy, and surgery may disrupt the balance. The suction device may pick up a normally benign strain of bacteria and introduce it into the uterus during the surgery. If that bug is *Clostridium*, a toxin-producing bacteria that disrupts normal cells, and if it materializes in excess, the spread could be dire. Mortuary workers call it "tissue gas"; its effect on dead bodies can be halted only by embalming.

When gas gangrene affects an organ, the odds of survival are grim—the mortality rate is as high as eighty percent.

If the young woman waiting for us in the room has gas gangrene, our only lifesaving measure will be to remove her uterus. Performing a hysterectomy in time, before the gangrenous tissue has the chance to spread to other organs, more vital organs, could save her life. In an older woman, the decision would be simple, but in a twenty-six-year-old who has never had children, whose future fertility hangs in the balance, the decision feels much more complex, more profound.

"They're ready for us." Rebecca pokes her head out of the operating door. The patient lies asleep, a tube down her throat to provide oxygen to her lungs, IV lines administering fluids, medications. Her face is young and unblemished. A tiny flower tattoo peeks from her shoulder.

"Hey, Dr. A?" A nurse snaps me alert. "We're ready to do our prep."

Before she bathes the patient's body in an orange stain of Betadine soap, I put on purple gloves to do my own exam. I step in between her legs and gently place my fingers inside. My other hand slides down from her sternum, slowly feeling for the top of her uterus. As I press with my top hand, I feel what I have never felt before, have only read about in texts as a medical student. I wonder whether I am imagining it, but as I press again, I am sure. Actual air bubbles crackle between my hands. A very subtle *pop! pop!* I step away from the bed, withdrawing my hands quickly. The blood flowing to my face does a precipitous dive down to my feet in that moment. I feel dizzy for a split second and step back far from the table. I peel off my gloves and stand staring at the patient's body.

Air bubbles within the cavity of the body are sinister and unwelcome visitors. The bubbles can be caused by dead tissue creating gaseous fumes—fumes that have no place within our organs. While we had been discussing the possibility of gas gangrene, up until that moment it had been theoretical, a possibility. When the air bubbles popped between my hands, my body knew it was true.

A routine abortion turned septic, bacteria turned noxious, and a healthy young woman lies on the precipice. Our role in saving her is crystal clear. An overwhelming sensation of responsibility and sadness sets in. We will take out her uterus and hopefully save her life. We will *have* to take out her uterus and hope we are in time to save her life.

Rebecca discusses the case with anesthesia while two nurses cleanse the patient's abdomen, using Q-tips to remove lint from her belly button, and shave bits of her pubic hair. The anesthesiologist, an experienced doctor in his sixties, stands at her head, monitoring vital signs and securing electrodes to her chest.

"I felt crackles," I say to him. Three words that tell a story. To him, my colleague, my senior in rank, that is all I need to say.

His eyebrows raise and he pauses. "That's not good," he replies.

"Not good," I repeat.

Gas gangrene. The words repeat themselves as orange-brown soap dries, as Rebecca and I scrub to our elbows. We walk into the operating room like surgeon zombies, our arms at ninety-degree angles. We dry off with sterile towels and allow ourselves to be gowned and gloved. We place blue surgical drapes over the patient, leaving a square window into her lower abdomen.

I hear Rebecca announce the name of the patient. Her name is the name of a stranger. I hear her name, and a new thought enters my mind—this case is the case of my grandmother. Abortion. Sepsis. Gangrene. Mehry's story reveals itself to me in this room.

I shake my head to clear the thought and focus back on Rebecca. She has the room's attention and details the procedure. We will attempt to find other sources for her sepsis, she says. We will look in her bladder. We will inspect her bowels. If we don't find any other injury, if there is no other explanation for why she is so sick, we will take out her uterus. We will remove her opportunity for a future pregnancy in exchange for saving her life. We will do this methodically and without regret, I think to myself. We will take the chance that we were wrong. We will wait several days until the pathology returns to know whether we did the right thing, but we will proceed with a certain knowing sense. We will tie together the clinical picture with the crackling we felt between our fingers.

Light music, surfer music, comes out of the Bluetooth speaker in the corner, and I serve as an assistant to Rebecca. My goal is to be the best possible assistant, to offer her suggestions if needed, to retract tissue so we can visualize what we need in an optimal way. I am alert and engaged. We talk through every decision. The camera is snaked into her bladder and her bladder looks perfect. No defect. Nothing strange there. We move into her abdomen. With a couple of swift slices of a scalpel we are deep into her belly. We have passed the thin layer of subcutaneous fat, sliced her shiny, white fascia, separated her gleaming red and taut rectus muscles, created a hole in her peritoneum, and we are staring face-to-face with her intestines.

The intestines are infinite. They loop and wind and take up most of the space within the belly. It is plausible that over the course of an abortion procedure an instrument could puncture through the uterus and poke a hole in the intestine. This would cause a leak of bowel contents, and a person might get very sick—septic, even, like our patient. We study inch after inch of intestine; we use a hand-over-hand method and run through her entire bowel. We squint and peer and look for any evidence of perforation. Her belly is clean. We don't smell feces. We don't see the greenish sign of stool leak. But we are diligent. If there is a hole in her bowel, maybe we can save her uterus. Maybe that will explain her infection. The bowel leak can be fixed, and she will recover. Her fertility will be preserved. Her future life choices will not be forever impacted by our actions.

"Nothing," Rebecca says after our exhaustive search. "Her bowels look perfect." I nod in agreement. We are checking down our list. Bladder—check. Bowels—check. We pause for a moment and talk to each other over the patient's body. Our hair, faces, and bodies are completely covered by sterile blue material. I can only see her eyes and she mine. We talk muffled through our masks. It might be an awkward scene for a passerby. The draped woman on the table. The abdomen cut open and intestines exposed. Instruments entering the body, IV lines flowing. Jack Johnson on the speakers. But this scene is my life's backdrop.

I stand with my gloved hands resting on the blue drapes that cover the patient's body. We gently return her bowels back into her belly cavity. Rebecca pulls out a larger retractor and starts attaching it to the table. "Okay," she calls out to the room. "We are going to do a hysterectomy."

There is an increased flutter of activity as instrument packages get torn open and nurses hand off clamps and scissors to the waiting scrub tech. Sutures get counted out loud and sponges used to wipe away blood are stacked and arranged on the sterile table.

Rebecca and I identify the structures we will need to clamp, cut through, and suture to enable the uterus to be removed in its entirety. The cardinal ligaments. The round ligament. The utero-ovarian. We will take out her fallopian tubes too. We pause at her ovaries. We will leave behind her ovaries. Perhaps the genetic code that resides within them will have a future one day. Technology can allow this. The removal of a single egg by a slim and precise instrument might salvage her potential for a biological child in the future. In this moment, her future is unclear, but we will allow her this decision. We pick up each perfect, shiny white ovary, and with reverence place them back into their rightful positions.

While operating, we talk, always letting the other one know what we are doing next.

"I'm going to clamp here, okay?" I say to Rebecca, poising my instrument around the biggest blood supply to the uterus, the uterine artery.

"Perfect," she responds.

We operate like extensions of each other, hoping that two brains, four hands, and twenty fingers will serve our patient better than each of us individually. We cut and we clamp, and we each tie down the suture material on our own side to keep another vessel sealed.

We then travel deep in the tunnel of her pelvis to operate along her cervix until we reach its junction with the vagina. We clamp across this base, and, with one swift cut of our scissors, the womb is amputated from her body and placed in a bucket next to our table.

I sigh out loud as we look at our patient, stable, on the table. The surgery is over. Her incision is closed with a neat line of staples—a Frankenstein smile across her lower abdomen. The anesthesiologist confirms that her vital signs are normal, she does not have a fever. Her blood loss was minimal.

We know that it will be several days before we learn the verdict. Normal uterus? Gangrenous tissue? We will wonder and wait. We remove our soiled surgical gowns. We walk out of the OR, and Rebecca heads down the hallway to talk to the family. She explains the need to have removed the uterus. She expresses hope that their daughter, their sister, their friend will now quickly recover. She emphasizes that the ovaries remain intact. If there is a desire for biological babies one day, there might be a way. For now, the patient is stable. Recovery is likely. The patient's parents lean into her words. Her mother's hand is clenched into a fist. When Rebecca finishes talking, the mother lets out a sigh and releases a tired smile. Still worried, but now there is some relief.

We meet in the locker room and change out of our scrubs and into our daytime clothes, then step into the light of the afternoon. The sun is bright, and the weekend is beginning. Rebecca and I pause for a moment next to our cars. We say quietly what we have said a dozen times that day: It was the right thing to do. Hopefully now she will get better.

"You did the right thing," I say to her straight. "I am proud of you."

It is a true but worried sentiment. I hope we did, in fact, think of everything.

When Rebecca calls me the following Monday evening to share the final pathology report, I am at home, sitting on my couch. My daughter is watching TV while my son types on his laptop. I am between them with a blanket on my lap, using this time as an excuse to sit near them both. I feel my daughter's leg sneak underneath the blanket and her cold toes shock my own warm thigh. My son has turned his screen toward me, and like a silent film, I watch his mouth explaining his game to me, but I cannot hear the words.

"Myonecrosis invading over half of the uterus," Rebecca says over the phone. "It could only have been due to something like *Clostridium*."

Gas gangrene. I felt it in my fingers, the pop of her uterus between my hands.

"The patient is doing really well," she continues. "She is probably going home tomorrow."

I nod and then speak to assure her I am still on the phone.

"Whoa," I say. "She would have died, Rebecca. She would have died."

I hang up the phone, reach for my daughter's toes, and squeeze them to warmth. The noxious sensation of *Clostridium* had been just underneath our young patient's skin. The through line from her to Mehry feels as connected as a single pulse.

Ghost Womb

2023

Our gas gangrene patient had been very sick, teetering close to death, just days after an abortion. And it's not just abortion that can lead to this; any pregnancy where there is an interruption to normal tissue within the uterus—from a vaginal bacterium or an invasive procedure, or if the water sac around the baby breaks or a fetus dies—can lead to a uterine infection, which, if left untreated, will spread. Sepsis is the shutting down of bodily organs—the kidneys stop working, the heart is affected, the liver and lung functions become impaired. For some women, this leads to blood-clotting and can cause a stroke in the brain that leads to blindness and death.

Our patient's situation was rare, unusual, highly unlikely. I spent days reliving the operation—the careful inspection of organs, the attempt to preserve her uterus. A case like this, a once-in-a-lifetime occurrence, will capture surgeons, remind us of our early days of training, when every scenario was imagined and practiced, if just through textbooks and in our heads. But there was more, I kept thinking. The reliving was about more than a medical fascination. I also kept remembering the night at my parents' house several years earlier, when I was seated on the floor with my mother, aunt, and uncle, asking them how Mehry died.

It was only after my father turned his attention away that night, and my mother stood up to clear the dishes, that my aunt Nargess motioned at me. She stepped outside for a cigarette and whispered for me to join her. She told me what the women of their village had told her—that Mehry was not prepared for a fifth baby in six years. That she might have tried to resolve the situation on her own.

"She drank a drink," Nargess whispered to me, cigarette breath between our faces close together. She was not supposed to be smoking, and she was not supposed to be telling me this detail.

"Something about drinking that drink. It killed her."

The answer was inside the uterus I removed with my hands.

When Mehry drank the herbal concoction to end her pregnancy, it did not work right away. But eventually, the fetus did stop growing. And when she did not bleed, when she did not pass the pregnancy, her uterus became infected. Then septic. Sepsis led to stroke. Stroke led to her death.

For Mehry, day 120 of the *Ruh* came and went, and nothing happened. She waited for the pains to come. She checked for spots of blood in her underwear, in the toilet. Nothing. Her belly swelled and grew, and after a few weeks of this Mehry had to accept that the tea had not worked. *Ruh* had come and gone. She decided that there was really nothing much more for her to do about the matter. She could not discuss it. Nobody, except for Nilufar and the aunties, knew. She resolved this by choosing a different day to bathe. She could not bear to be in front of them at this point. Her pregnancy was now apparent to the world—her belly button pushing outward, her legs widening to accommodate her walk. She slept more at night now and rose more slowly in the mornings.

Seven months into the pregnancy her muscles felt heavy, her ankles like lead. Walking into the bedroom, she felt the pulsing in her temples of a headache about to start. She drank a glass of water and splashed some on her face. Placed one hand on her belly. When was the last time she had felt the baby move? It had been a long day, busy with the children. In all of it, she had not paid attention to movement. She poked into her belly gently and said a few words: "Wake up, wake up." This usually worked to ignite the series of kicks and pokes that accompanied her throughout the day and night. But right now, nothing. She pushed her finger into her belly another time. Again, nothing.

Mehry moved to her bed and lay on her side. With both hands cupping the pregnancy, she felt for the undulations she always felt while falling asleep. An almost rhythmic rocking, as if the baby was finding its own sleep position. Or had baby hiccups, like in her other pregnancies. The hiccups always seemed to happen at night. A quick spasm that she could time like the seconds on a clock. *Tick tick, tick tick.* But again, silence. She shifted positions, from right to left, sitting to standing. All of the motions she knew so well from her pregnancies before. Minutes passed and turned to hours. She knew, but she did not want to know: the baby was gone. She felt it so deeply that she at once let out a wail. The baby was gone. No longer moving. No longer growing. It had not passed when she wanted it to, but now her punishment was this. An almost fully grown baby. Dead on the inside.

Mehry spoke to no one about the baby. She went about her days with the measured and automatic motions of a practiced woman. Smile for the children. Cook basic but delicious meals. Brush her hair. Wash her face. At first, she thought she was mistaken. A few mornings in a row she thought she felt the baby stir inside, and hope filled her, only to deflate when she realized it was a gas bubble or a tightening of the uterus. Weeks passed and her belly did not grow. She did not expect anybody to notice, and she was right. The help went about their chores, treating her with kindness and offering extra assistance. Her husband found a reputable nanny and would introduce them when the delivery date got closer. The children tickled and danced, jumped and played. They created an ambience of normalcy around her. As long as she could hear their voices and touch their skin, she was still alive, although the death within left her feeling like an apparition.

What happens to the vessel carrying a ghost? she wondered. Knowing that she harbored a dead baby, likely dead from drinking the poison tea, slowly and deliberately drained her of any vital essence she had remaining. Her skin grew pale, her lips thin, her eyes wider and more deeply set. When she caught a glimpse of herself in the mirror she thought, I look like the ghost that I am.

"Mehry *jan*." Her husband entered the kitchen early one morning. "The men will be coming over tonight," he reminded her.

"*Baleh janam*, yes, dear," Mehry answered. Her voice sounded heavy to her. This morning it felt harder to get out of bed and her movements in the kitchen were slowed.

"*Halet khoobeh?* Are you feeling okay?" For a moment her husband paused and stared into her face. "You look tired."

"No, no, I'm okay. I'll be fine." Mehry looked away from his face and moved toward the stove, prepared to pour him his glass of tea.

"I will get more help for tonight. This pregnancy is wearing you out," he said, and reached out and placed a hand on each of her shoulders, tipping his head down to place a kiss on her forehead. The move was so tender, so unexpected, that Mehry felt a tightness in her throat and a sting in her eyes.

"*Merci*, thank you," she said softly, and moved away. They had spoken so little that entire year. But Mehry would never ask for more. She deserved whatever she got from this marriage. She drank poison and killed her baby. Whatever came her way, she deserved.

"I will be back tonight." He carried his tea glass out of the kitchen and down the hall, and Mehry listened to the thud of his footsteps. When to tell him that something was wrong? She wondered this every moment of every day since she realized the baby had died. He might not recover from the news. As busy as he was, as much as he traveled, she knew this much—the children were his heart as much as they were hers. Everything he did he did for them. She knew he had already imagined their life with the next baby. The next baby. Just the image of the next baby—lifeless, pulseless—sent a pain to her head and she pushed her palm onto her forehead to make it go away.

Mansour and Mahshid entered the kitchen, and she looked at

them and smiled. Something is wrong, she thought. The head pain had not subsided; instead, she felt it move behind her eyes and for a moment her vision was blurred. First the children looked fuzzy, and then it looked like there were two of each of them.

"Good morning, *maman*!" Mansour moved in for a kiss and Mahshid touched her leg.

"Good morning, my little hearts," Mehry said as she gently guided each of them toward the table, one hand on each of their backs, more to help keep herself steady than to move them.

The nanny entered the kitchen with Nargess and Mohsen, and Mehry stared at her, hoping her look alone would signal her to take over. The nanny was also fuzzy, and when Mehry closed her eyes she heard a ringing in her ears.

"Mrs. Abedi, you don't look well," the nanny said as she reached out a hand and grasped Mehry's. Her hand felt cool and Mehry realized her own was warm and sweaty.

"I think I just need to lie down," Mehry answered. She kissed the little ones on their cheeks and slowly walked toward her bedroom. While she walked, she heard the children's voices. They sounded muddled but happy. They are happy, she thought to herself as she laid herself on top of her covers. Thanks to God, the children are happy.

Mehry slept and slept and while she slept, she dreamt a dream that was vivid and full of life. She saw herself flying. She knew that she was the front of a V-shaped migration, like the gulls she watched fly south every fall. Her arms floated out as wings and her hair flowed behind her as a sail. As she flew, she glanced right, and then left, peering over her shoulder to make sure the others followed. Mansour on one side. Mahshid on the other. Nargess so close to Mahshid's feet the draft kept them connected as one. Mohsen perched on her back and strapped to her front; wrapped in cheesecloth and protected with her chest was the baby. Sleeping. But breathing. Pink and alive.

For the longest time, Mehry flew. It was as if she never needed her feet to touch land again. When she dipped and dove to avoid other birds, when she swooped close to point out a waterfall or a bear fishing for salmon in a river, she heard the whooping of her children. Their delight. For a certain amount of time, they flew in silence. The earth went still, but there was just enough wind to allow them each to glide, arms out, chins forward. Below, just a billow of white clouds. Sugar cubes transformed to their most cotton-like state. There were no obstacles here. There was no fear. Somehow, she felt her purpose in that moment. The guide. The protector.

Even while she slept, a part of her knew she was dreaming. And in the space between sleep and waking a gust of wind blew through her. She felt her body shake and lose its balance. She held the baby tight to her chest and yelled to Mohsen to hold on tight. She felt that he was losing his grip, and as his hand slipped away, she spun in circles from the force of losing him to the fall. The other children watched from behind. They slowed their flight. Paused. She heard their yelps and yelled at them to go. "Go get Mohsen," she cried. She watched them, now three but blurred together into one, diving through the clouds where Mohsen had disappeared. She tumbled, spun, dizzied out of control.

"Mrs. Abedi, Mrs. Abedi, are you okay?"

She heard the voice of the nanny and blinked her eyes. Everything was blurry. The light coming in through the window. Her hands that shook in her lap. The face of the woman stroking her back, putting a wet cloth to her forehead, blurry, waving.

The bedsheets, along with her nightgown, skin, and hair, were soaked in sweat. Mehry shivered and her bones hurt with the force of her trembling.

"Just a dream, just a bad dream." She instinctively placed her hand on her belly to feel for movement. It was firm and painful. Just to touch her skin hurt. And the baby was still there. There, but not there.

"*Merci*, thank you, I'm okay." She turned to the nanny, handed back the wet towel. It was already warm. Despite her shivers, her face radiated heat like the sun. Burning. Her eyes stinging. The whole room went in and out of focus, the light like a dim haze.

"The guests will be here, Mrs. Abedi," the nanny spoke carefully. "Can I help you get dressed?"

The men. Her husband's gathering that they had meticulously planned. Drinks and tea in the courtyard because the weather was unusually warm. Then dinner inside. All of the usual dishes. *Khoresh bademjan*, with the eggplants. *Zereshk polo*, with the sour berries. Lamb kebabs. Tomato and cucumber salad.

"I will get dressed, thank you." Mehry motioned the nanny out of the room and stood up. Her head pounded, now not just in the temples but inside the entire right side of her head and down her back. It is a migraine messing with the eyes, she told herself. A cup of tea will help.

She dressed in the flowing white dress she had picked out for tonight—simple, comfortable, and pretty against her skin. Her husband liked that dress, complimented her every time she wore it. And it was loose enough to keep the size of her belly unseen. Nobody could question how far along she was or whether she looked too big or too small for the due date.

"Mehry *jan*, are you okay? I heard you were not feeling well." Her husband stepped in toward her. He had three faces but otherwise looked good. Handsome. Clean-shaven and wearing one of his favorite suits. Always in a tailored suit.

"I'm okay, I'm okay," she repeated. "Just a bad dream. Are we ready?"

"We will be outside." He pecked her cheek, and she could smell his skin, so clean. Soap and aftershave. Cigar and a hint of whiskey. As if she had never smelled it before. She closed her throbbing eyes and took in a deep breath. Her chest was tight, and she realized she could not inhale all the way. Just sadness, she thought. My chest holding in the sadness.

It was a festive scene in the courtyard. Lights twinkled around the perimeter and a fire in the pit crackled and centered the men, who sat on benches and stools. The conversation sounded light with laughter. Thigh-slapping. Arms around shoulders. She always liked nights like this when the whole house felt alive. The children ran in circles around the men. They poked sticks into the fire and waved them to the sky, watching sparks fly off and float past the trees.

"*Befarmaeed*, help yourself." Mehry had taken the tray of tea from the cook in the kitchen. Tea glasses filled with the steaming liquid of scented rosewater and cardamom lined the tray. Each glass with its own tiny saucer and miniature gold spoon. Sugar cubes that sat in an adjacent crystal bowl.

Passing out the tea was a ritual she enjoyed. Doing it perfectly was the mark of a true Iranian woman. Bride material, her grandmother used to say. Start with the eldest man first, she was coached. And then down in age from there. Keep the tray still. Turn slightly to offer the sugar cubes. Laugh or smile or accept whatever flattery comes your way. This tea-serving routine, it is your time to shine.

Tonight, she found it difficult to balance the tray. She felt unsteady. And the eyes had not recovered. In the dusk light everything looked dark. She even thought, as she stepped outside, that she could no longer see out of her left eye. Just a blackness out of that side and a blurriness on the other. She walked toward the men's voices and the light from the fire. She knew this part well. The eldest man would be closest to the door, and she would head there first. She walked and heard the clinking of the glasses against one another. Her hands shook and she tried to focus on the tray to keep from spilling.

"*Bah, bah, che khanoum, che chai.* Wow, what a woman! What tea!" Her husband sounded jovial and proud. She looked up and smiled and turned her body to face the elder man to her left.

"Mehry *jan*! Watch out!"

Her right ankle felt a sting and then a burn. She looked down to see flames at the bottom of her skirt, then noticed how close she had come to the fire. So close she was practically in the fire.

"Move away, move away!" she heard voices yell, and somebody grabbed the tray of tea. Four arms picked her up and carried her to a bench off the side of the yard. She felt a pain in her foot, so hot, so intense, it was as if each individual toenail were being pulled off. Her body, overtaken by the throbbing pulse of her temples, the darkness behind her eyes, the tautness of her belly, the burning leg, began to turn numb. She felt herself teetering and fought to keep her eyes awake.

"Water, water! Bring water."

The scene around her had so quickly changed that Mehry felt confused. The heat rose up her thigh and she could make out the orange flames that caught her skirt.

"Hurry, hurry!" There was now panic in her husband's voice, and in slow motion, Mehry turned to watch him tip a bucket over her, splashing her leg and dress with water. It was cold, but she barely felt the temperature. She blinked, confused, unable to discern the shadow of faces that surrounded her.

"We have to go," her husband called out. "We have to get her to the hospital."

She felt herself lifted off the ground, practically carried by her husband on one side, another man gripping her elbow on the other.

"To the car, to the car." Their voices were loud and distant at the same time.

There was no more time left for precautions. Her white dress flowed; its edges singed with the char from the fire. Mehry felt her hair blow behind her and outstretched her arms. From there she was lifted and her feet left the ground, never to touch down again.

(We watched her get taken away, my mother tells me today. My brother and I saw the whole thing. The skirt catching on fire. The water putting it out. The men lifting her up in her white dress. She was already an angel floating away.)

I'm flying, she thought, a weightlessness taking over. It's finally happening. I can fly.

Woman, Life, Freedom

2022

Mehry's death did to the family what the loss of the mother always does—cratered a hole in those left behind. The unborn baby died with her, and then, unexpectedly, unfathomably, the one-year-old brother died within the year. My grandfather remarried and his last bride introduced my father to the family—they were cousins. When my mother turned sixteen and my father was recruited to finish his medical training in the United States, they married and moved across the world. The plan was always to return, and they tried. With my brother and me in tow, my parents moved back to Shiraz in 1976 to raise us. Iran was home to their native language and culture, where each had eight siblings and friends and dreams of us all growing up in community. The richness of the culture was not lost on me, even at a young age. Poetry, joke-telling, pots of bubbling stew, an open door to visitors, the smell of warm saffron sprinkled on basmati rice—they defined my early childhood. Those days, I spoke Farsi, I was called Fariba, my Persian birth name, and my memories of this time—lodged in a series of photos, stories, and sense—are these: men's and women's voices mixed, my mother with piles of hair atop her head, my aunties lining their eyes with charcoal flecked with blue, singing and dancing, dancing and laughing, laughing and talking late into the night.

We left Iran in 1978 with thousands of others. The rumblings of regime change, the prediction that an extremist Islamic government would take over, was enough to prompt my parents to make the decision so many made at that time—to pack up minimal belongings and find a new country to call home. If survivor guilt is the result of living when others have perished, then leaving guilt is the result of dreaming of a different future for your children—more opportunity, more freedom—and being right.

We witnessed the violent installation of Supreme Leader Ayatollah Khomeini from the comfort of our suburban living room, drinking tea sweetened by sugar cubes and answering middle-of-the-night calls from relatives on our dial phone. A confusion interrupts the childhood of many first-generation kids—Where do we belong? To which country do we hold an allegiance? The chants of "Death to America" on the nightly news peppered the background of my dinners, but otherwise, my life progressed exactly as hoped. A girl in California has every opportunity in the world, my father used to say. And for me, he was right. Piano lessons, dance classes, swim team, ski weekends—my privilege abounded while my cousins lived with air-raid sirens, shuttered schools, and the threat of bombardment for the nearly eight years of the Iran-Iraq War. When I graduated from college, Silicon Valley boomed opportunity for my classmates, and many of my friends became overnight millionaires. Equally educated graduates from engineering and doctorate programs in Iran struggled to survive financially under strict economic sanctions.

It was only as I grew older, had children of my own, that the realization set in: my fearless American indignation over personal freedom, my staunch defense of the First Amendment and reproductive rights—they were gifted to me, and my future children, at three years old, when my parents filed us onto an airplane and said goodbye to their past lives. It is an autonomy we take for granted, even while witnessing our friends and family attempt parallel lives in Iran. They too study for exams. They too dream of marriage equality. They too perform surgery and care for pregnant women. The thread lines of our DNA are practically the same; her eyes look like my eyes. And yet when female doctors like me, in major cities such as Tehran and Shiraz, leave their homes for work in the hospital, they are forced to cover their bodies and hair under the threat of arrest, and now death.

On October 1, 2022, more than a half million people around the world, from Los Angeles to Toronto to Rome to Lebanon, gathered in unity and chanted the same few words—"Mahsa Amini." "Woman, Life, Freedom." "*Zan, Zendegi, Azadi.*" By then, hundreds of Iranians had been killed and twenty thousand arrested on the seventeenth day of explosive protest in that country after a young woman, Jina Mahsa Amini, was tortured and killed by the Islamic Revolutionary Guard for showing a few tendrils of hair from underneath her headscarf.

Many of us did not stop staring at our phones for a month. For four weeks we watched the videos streaming in, despite the Iranian government's attempt to shut down communication. Women spun off their headscarves and tossed them into the fire. One grandmother defiantly sat with her bare head, taunting the surrounding armed police. We sent each other texts and Instagram messages—**Can you believe what is happening?** We had witnessed uprisings in the past—protests against election results, economic sanctions—but we had never seen this. A blatant, literal flipping-off of the regime—fourteen-year-old girls screaming "Death to the Dictator," women walking arm in arm with long hair down their backs. The simplest images of a girl showing her hair in public circulated and we could not look away. It had been decades since we had seen a woman's hair on the streets of Tehran, and we knew that they were unveiling at the risk of their own lives. A twenty-two-year-old removed her headscarf, tied up her blond hair in a bun, and was hit by six bullets within minutes. A seventeen-year-old cut her hair short and stepped forward into the crowd. They murdered her too.

Those of us in the Iranian diaspora knew the crackdown would be brutal and yet, this time, nobody seemed to retreat. My aunt lost access to WhatsApp and we lost contact for a week. One night, at 4:00 a.m. her time, she saw the bars reappear on her phone and immediately called to let us know she was okay. Teenagers posted videos from bedrooms and begged us to share. They are killing us in the streets, they said. Where is the world? they asked. Then the clerical regime's security forces trapped and locked students in the parking lot of the Sharif University of Technology, firing live ammunition and arresting students—the brightest of the bright, the MIT of Iran, it is called. Eliminate the future, erase all hope; that's what I think of this tactic. Instead, the young generation is stepping forward, flipping over portraits of the supreme leader in their classrooms. This is what bravery looks like, we say, and we are in awe. As Iranians, we might have been them once, but today, they are one and their own.

The month the world began chanting Mahsa Amini's name, my own divorce was under way. The dynamic between me and Keith, the synchronicity we performed as parents, had broken down. Input from the outside world abounded. It is the right thing to do. It is the worst thing you could do. Why are you doing this? It does makes sense, you being a doctor and so busy and such. You're a doctor, you should know that it will ruin the kids. Leave now. Stay longer. I'm so sorry. So sorry. So many sorries.

I moved out of the family home I thought would be ours forever. For a few weeks, in preparation to leave and settle into a small place just down the street, I tried and failed to buy furniture, bedding, kitchen utensils. I melted down inside of department stores. I sank into couches and could barely stand back up. I walked around shops and filled carts only to leave them against a wall and walk out. Woman, life, freedom took on new meaning for me—my work, my marriage, my own invisible inheritance. I had choice, though. I had all the choices.

In the midst of viewing the videos, reading the articles, sleeping on a new mattress, using rental apartment dishes, I walked into a tattoo parlor down the street from my new home and within an hour *Zan, Zendegi, Azadi*—Woman, Life, Freedom—was tattooed on my forearm. My first tattoo, my only. It was an entitled act of defiance, this I knew, to raise my left fist in solidarity with those words etched in ink. In that moment, even in the shadow of *Dobbs*, the words felt more like metaphor than reality. My quest for freedom was simply an internalized one.

My father seemed to reinforce this by refusing to believe the tattoo was real.

"That's not permanent, is it?" he asked the next time he saw me. He put on his reading glasses and pulled my arm toward him so he could examine it.

"Oh yes, it is real," I answered, flexing my forearm closer.

"Not forever," he said, still staring. "It's the temporary kind, isn't it? It will wash off eventually."

"Oh no." I laughed. "This is forever."

"No, no," he repeated, unwavering.

I rolled my sleeve down to spare him from having to keep looking at it. Here was the man who had done everything to secure my freedom over his lifetime. But only I had grown up in America and it was obvious, our different ideas about acts of resistance and unforgivable transgression.

"Ha, you're right, Dad. It's not permanent. It is the wash-off kind. After six weeks, it is gone."

Wash-off tattoo is the henna on Navid's bald scalp. Four years into her diagnosis of ovarian cancer, her hair has fallen out and grown back in three times. It has been blond and blue, spiked and curly. Today it is gone again, smooth and shaved, ready for another surgery, another series of chemotherapy appointments. Navid is a Harvard scientist who works at the Dana-Farber Cancer Institute.

There is no question that her survival, her beating the odds of surviving stage four ovarian cancer, lies partly in the ongoing research of her institution—every time we think there is nothing left to be done, something new and miraculous is discovered to extend her life.

I lay next to her as the henna artist we hired began painting dark-brown leaves onto the round orb of her head. We asked for pomegranates, our favorite fruit, our Persian identifier. "Connect the pomegranates with flowers and swirls," I requested.

Navid had eventually chosen not to hide her baldness after purchasing expensive wigs, trying on scarves and baseball caps. Something about feeling bold in her aliveness. Something about taking ownership of her own loss, the loss of identity she had felt with her long, dark hair. Ironically or not, it coincided with the ferocious attacks on hair that instigated Iranians' chants of "*Zan, Zendegi, Azadi*." We had been texting and talking, sending videos and messages of grief and hope since the uprisings began. Her surgery playlist included the new freedom anthem out of Iran, "Baraye," a beautiful symbol of protest streaming out of car windows and whose songwriter, Shervin Hajipour, had been sentenced to prison for writing.

In her past surgeries, she was accompanied first by a Barack Obama doll, traded in for a Ruth Bader Ginsburg doll, and now, tomorrow, it would be just she alone, her head gorgeously inscribed with the ancient symbols of life from our shared history.

In Iran, the marching, the horn honking, the surrounding of prisons, these continued for nearly a year, longer than anyone anticipated. My American friends would ask me to explain what was going on, not quite grasping the stakes of the uprising. I'd answer—these are the loud, unified gasps of air from a population that has been holding its breath for forty years. These are the actions of a people who know what freedom is and can be—bodily autonomy, the right of women to choose their clothing, the human need to express itself without fear of deadly repercussion.

Witness this moment for what it is, I tried to explain. When a misogynist, violent, authoritarian government regulates the movement, the activity, the choices of women, blood will eventually be shed. The people of Iran are an educated, literate, mobilized population who remember what it felt like to have wind in their hair and fingers interlocked walking down the street. They are us.

I researched recent Iranian history as it unfolded in my lifetime, and I also remembered: just the other day I was able to perform my job as a gynecologist without threat of repercussion. It was practically yesterday that *I* was not afraid. The tides, the optics, they can be swift and unyielding. What was taken for granted one day is just as quickly taken away.

Healthcare Is Healthcare

2025

On the one-year anniversary of the death of Jina Mahsa Amini, a small group of Iranians marched in Portland. I hung large banners honoring the Woman, Life, Freedom movement on the mobile clinic, and left it parked along the route of the march. When we passed by the RV, we all cheered.

On the two-year anniversary, we were on the eve of electing a new president, and the stakes felt higher than ever. In the weeks after the presidential election of 2024, I rediscovered one of my favorite aspects of hospital medicine—no matter your politics, no matter your beliefs, we care for patients equally and without judgment. Identities shed themselves with the clothing people are forced to remove when they are admitted. We meet each other in gowns and scrubs, expressing similar pains, fears, and questions.

One morning while working a shift at a hospital, I was called up to the intensive care unit almost immediately after arriving. A patient had been admitted overnight who was in her second trimester of pregnancy and her organs were failing. The doctors in the unit explained that she had presented overnight almost in a coma, and they were struggling to maintain her blood pressure despite multiple medications.

I quickly reviewed her chart in the computer and learned a few key details—she was twenty weeks pregnant; she had a serious underlying medical condition that she had lived with since childhood. For most of her adult life her doctors cautioned her that pregnancy had a very high possibility of killing her—the strain of a growing fetus would likely be too hard on her organs, and they cautioned her to use birth control or consider permanent sterilization.

Like most of us, and especially those who have not been raised in a medical family and received a medical degree, the details of the what-ifs can often defy understanding. This patient, and her husband, desperately wanted a family, and they had made the decision to become pregnant. She did not believe the worst-case scenario would happen to her; she believed she would fall into the category of "miracle." Now, at twenty weeks, a gestational age that is too early for a baby to survive, she was dying.

I met the couple at the bedside. The patient was puffy with fluid under her skin—her face, arms, and legs appeared waterlogged, and she could barely keep her eyes open from the effort. Her husband stood next to her, had one hand on her arm, and looked at me, worried. I did what I always do when a conversation is going to be difficult, complicated, emotional—I took a seat on the edge of the bed, carved out a little place for myself in their space. This is important, I truly believe, to help patients understand that what we are doing involves them and me—we are a team and in this work as a team there cannot be an us and a them. Medical decision-making is often multifaceted, it is complex, and it is always, always individual. To determine what course of intervention to take, one must consider the patients first, their unique set of physical circumstances, and then all the other components that are important to them—priorities, faith, family, and so on.

"Do you feel like you understand what is going on?" I looked to the patient and then to her husband. It did not escape me that a presidential election had just occurred, and half the country had voted to possibly make abortion illegal under any circumstance. I knew that this couple, this husband might well have cast his vote in that direction.

The patient nodded her head and used clear language to explain back to me what was happening. She had been aware of her medical condition most of her life. She was told that becoming pregnant might endanger her health. She had not wanted to believe it. She had really hoped to have this baby. But right then, she felt like she was dying. She actually said that she knew that she could die, she felt it in the swelling all over her body and the way her heart felt heavy as it tried to pump blood.

I looked to her husband and asked him the same question. He nodded back and said, "I don't want her to die. Whatever we have to do, please don't let her die."

I have served on medical committees within hospitals for nearly twenty years. In these meetings, administrators without medical degrees sit with physicians and together try to align goals. These include measures to increase quality of care, improve safety for patients, and also reduce costs and consider bottom line. Often these discussions are difficult, since healthcare is an unpredictable service and does not always fit traditional business models. I have also spoken to legislators in town hall meetings, in boardrooms, and at negotiation tables. I always invite them to do one thing before coming to a conclusion about policy decisions—put on a pair of scrubs and spend twenty-four hours in the hospital with me. Sit on the edge of the bed for these conversations. Step into our shoes and then meet me back at the table.

"I can explain it like this." I had one hand on the patient now too. "If you stay pregnant, your health is likely to get worse. You are on every possible medication right now and they are not working—the strain on your organs from the pregnancy is impossible to overcome. If you were further along, we could deliver the baby and do everything to keep it alive, but as you know, at twenty weeks, if we deliver the baby, it will not survive."

The patient and her husband looked at each other and I felt a sting in my own eyes when I saw theirs get wet.

"But the reality is this," I continued. "If we keep you pregnant in order to try to save the baby, there is a high chance that you will die. And when you die, the baby will also die."

Pause.

Pause.

Pause.

I feel a visceral aversion to slogans on the topic of abortion—labels such as "pro-choice" and "pro-life," words such as "murder," and also statements such as "abortion is healthcare." When

I listen to nonmedical lawmakers, politicians, or even laypeople debate abortion, I feel myself step away. It is an insult to women, and their loved ones, who make decisions around whether to end or continue a pregnancy to simplify the issue into words that can fit on bumper stickers. It is an affront to our shared humanity.

However, sitting on the bed, staring into the edematous face of this young patient, I repeated silently to myself the words "abortion is healthcare." It *is* healthcare. This situation is just one of hundreds of scenarios where women find themselves pregnant and in need of the opportunity to consider the impact on their lives. Simply maintaining a pregnancy is not the equivalent of life. Simply ending a pregnancy is not the equivalent of death.

"You don't have to make a decision right now." I knew this couple needed some time to process for themselves. "And I have also called our specialists—our high-risk doctor, our premature infant doctor. We are going to have them all come and speak to you. We will give you as much information as we can, and then, when you feel like you know what you want to do, we will be there for you. In the meantime, if you start getting worse, we will tell you that too."

We would. This is the part that many do not know, or see, or believe. That some of us physicians will not rest, not sleep, when there is a patient in crisis on the unit. That the agony of their situation seeps into our consciousness. That we also turn to our sense of morality, our faith, our experience to sit quietly in another room, pore over the literature, pray for a turn in her condition, make sure we have not left any options unexplored. We have committed ourselves to this work, and for most of us, it is the honor and duty of our lives.

Mama

2025

At first, our aim with the mobile clinic was to provide access—to create a model of care where everyone could see a specialist, no matter how physically or politically isolated they were. Over time, though, the mission of providing access expanded to include people who had other reasons to choose our clinic: A history of medical trauma, so they avoided walking through the doors of an office building or hospital. Neurodivergent patients who felt more comfortable in a smaller, private space. Transgender patients who were not quite sure how a traditional gynecology waiting room would view them. Young people who accompanied their friends, roommates, lovers for nonjudgmental sexually transmitted infection testing, birth control, emergency contraception, abortion guidance. And on and on.

One patient arrived with a notebook and a list of questions.

Aiden had been referred by their community of friends, a mix of cis and queer, nonbinary, trans, and straight, to discuss their need for gender-affirming care. But first they had some questions. They wanted to know what professional medical organizations I belonged to; they wanted to know whether I had experience with hormones and transgender care. I answered both questions, which prompted them to ask, "So, why did you choose this work? What made you care about providing gender-affirming care for transgender folks? Do you have a personal motivation?"

I paused. "Hmmm. Nobody has really asked me that before."

"I'm curious," they responded. "Because there are a lot of doctors not wanting to provide this care right now."

"Well," I started slowly, and closed my computer on my lap. I wanted to make sure I really said this correctly, truthfully.

"I can't speak for anybody else. But I know this much for me. . . ." My eyes drifted to the tattoo on my forearm.

"My parents left their country in order to provide me with a life where my autonomy was protected. Valued. Supported. Even encouraged," I continued. "And now, another version of me, the one that would still be there if my parents hadn't left, is being shot and killed in the streets for daring to show her hair." I listened to my own voice—I had never explained this before.

"This fight for bodily autonomy, it starts with one person, one torment. And if we do not stand for that, it spreads to all of us." I thought for a moment, then continued, "I only recently learned that my grandmother died as a result of attempting an illegal abortion. She left behind four young children. How different might things have been for her, for my family? We are only as free as each other is free. Do you know what I mean?"

Aiden nodded and closed their notebook. I was perched on a little stool. They were leaning toward me, listening from the couch. I smiled and said thank you. Like, really, thank you for those questions.

When I tell people about the mobile clinic there is a general excitement in how they respond. Many doctors and nurses express a genuine respect, even envy, of the model of care and how I spend my days. I describe the space—it is cozy, intimate, the fairy lights twinkle, and my own playlist of music is in the background. Sometimes we wrap up an anxious patient in a weighted blanket and pop them popcorn, or hand them a lollipop, while also discussing their care. Within the walls exists a shared humanity. I am their doctor. But on wheels, I am also their travel companion. We journey together in a way not conceivable in a traditional office setting or hospital.

And there are the parts that nobody knows. That I have yet to pay myself from the clinic. That despite how it looks from the outside, this project was self-funded and occasionally requires further dips into my personal savings to keep it going. That sometimes there is a perception of "doctor" that is far more glamorous than the emptying of gray water out the back of an RV, or washing grease from a generator off my hands before the day begins. That the smile that opens the door is genuine because most days I still can't believe patients trust us enough to step foot into this unconventional-looking place to undress and be their vulnerable selves. That I've cursed loudly as I've backed into buildings in the rain and accidentally shattered our windows, and cried occasionally when the power unexpectedly went out. But once the parking brake is on, the slides are expanded, the ultrasound machine is powered, and someone walks in for the first time, I reach out to them, often with a hug. I am more myself in this space—as the doctor I was never going to be, and was never more meant to be—than in any other space.

One night after parking the clinic, transferring to my car, dropping off labs and Pap smear samples into the pickup box on my front porch, I walk into the door of my house. The kids are teenagers now, busy with activities, and the front room is empty. I pause, remembering a similar night years ago when I entered to find my daughter, Naiya, twirling in circles as she spun around the living room. I watched her hair flip to catch up with the dimple on her cheek, her feet on tiptoes to spin her faster. She is four generations removed, I thought. From Mehry to Mahshid to me. From Afsar to my father. She is all of us in real-time motion. Her skirt fanned out and I saw my grandmother, serving tea to the men when she caught a flame. She stumbled and stopped herself and my mother was in labor with me. Naiya laughed, caught her breath, and looked up to see me watching.

"Mama!" she cried out, and ran to throw her arms around my waist.

"You." I put my hands on her shoulders and looked her in the eyes—dark, almond eyes.

"*You* are mine, forever and always mine." I drew her to my body and for a second, I felt the umbilical cord between us, the invisible string I described to her as always connecting us, even during the long hours we were apart.

She pulled away from my arms and leaned in to peck my cheek, a quick, compassionate gesture toward me.

"Mama," she said again, turning from me and walking away, with one glance backward. "I am my own."

Epilogue

Most mornings I wake without an alarm. In the summer months, it is with the first glimpse of light. In the winter, I force myself to get up before six, my "stolen hour," as I call it. It is a time when most others are sleeping, and if the sky is turning from gray to pink, or black to gray, warm or wet, it does not matter. I am outside by six. These days, I first have to detach my sleepy dog from my pajama bottoms before we head out, leash-less at first, and then leashed the closer we walk toward civilization, toward the dawn coffee-shop dwellers and our morning treats.

I spend this hour in the coffee shop with chitchat, checking bank accounts online, peeking at the hospital labor board to make sure there are no imminent emergencies. I catch up on the medical charts from my clinic, respond to questions from patients, and review the schedule for the day. We will be inserting two IUDs today, and I confirm that the patients received their overnight premedications for easier insertions. We will be counseling a few about menopause. One person thinks she is pregnant, early testing is positive. The schedule is full, the lunch hour is booked with two online meetings. The clinic will need to be parked in its assigned weekly location by nine o'clock sharp to be ready for our first patient at nine thirty.

Stolen hour pushes past its limit to seven thirty. I revel in the time spent in the back of the coffee shop, consider a second Americano, know that I need to head back to make sure the kids remember their one job—to ready themselves for school. When I get back home, my daughter is perfecting her hair. My son stays invisible until the last minute when he's due out the door. I am back on the computer. I keep the screen turned off, the voices from my colleagues in my ear as I also perfect my hair. I collect linens and shipped medications and lab supplies to take to the clinic. By eight fifteen I am in my car, headed toward the RV lot.

Because this is Portland, it is raining and wet. I have given up trying to stay dry. The gates to the parking lot are closed with a rusty chain lock and I hop out of the car, unlock the rolling gate, and push it open. It catches on pebbles and an overgrown thorny bush along the way. I lift it a bit, grunting and half-soaked when I return to my car, to pull it in and park. I bring the linens, medications, and lab supplies into the RV. Out go the dirty laundry, cardboard boxes, and trash.

Pulling out the RV requires one more hop out of the car past the damn gate, closing it shut, locking it tight, wiping wet hands on the cloth of the car seat before driving away. I have two stops before arriving to our clinic location—both are messy. First, I pull into a gas station to fill the tank as well as an extra gas can with 1.8 gallons. The onboard generator recently broke, and while I wait (and wait, and wait) for it to be repaired, I am using an external generator. It weighs either a hundred or ten thousand pounds and requires me to lift it in and out of the vehicle at the beginning and end of each day. It also drinks about 1.7 gallons of gas each clinic day, hence the extra can.

I put on pink exam gloves when filling the gas can. We all know no amount of scrubbing and Purell will completely eliminate the scent of fresh gasoline. Those gloves are tossed and replaced with a new pair when I pull into the sewage dump station. When it is still raining out, this next task feels like the ultimate reason to reconsider my life choices. I stand in the rain, connect the hose to the sewage tank drain system at the side of the truck, plunge the other end into a hole in the ground, and open: first the black water (unimaginable stench) rinsed clear with the gray water (soapy, bubbles). The hose is rinsed with fresh water, and I dispose of the gloves outside of the rig. This part of the process feels almost unmentionable.

Once we're parked at our assigned location, I wrestle with the substitute generator. I have developed a system of lowering it slowly down the three steps while resting a handle on my right shoulder. Two months into this system, I develop pretty severe upper back pain that takes me days to understand. (*Why does my back hurt so badly?* I ask everyone who is not a witness to these mornings.) The gas is poured in; the engine is fired up. Laura, my medical assistant, has joined me, and I connect my phone to Bluetooth. We hit play on the playlist and open up the RV slides.

This is when the day really begins. The sandwich boards welcoming our patients are set outside. The orange awning is unfurled and signals that we are open. The fairy lights are switched on and we can hear the rain hitting the ceiling. Laura sets out our plug-in fireplace display in the exam room—a new, cozy addition this past winter that outputs heat and crackles. I turn on my computer to view our schedule.

It is 9:29 a.m. A car pulls up in the parking space next to us. Laura sends the patient a text: **Come on in!** We open the door, and she steps inside and sits opposite me on the couch.

This much is clear—neither she nor I know how our stories will end. But this space, warm and cozy and functional, was created by us, for us. In here we have choices, and in here we have each other. For now, that is the story that matters. For this moment, that is enough.

Acknowledgments

I wrote this book in the cracks of my life, like the breath between labor contractions. Conception, gestation, three stages of labor and birth, postpartum, and, finally, forever. There is no birth without the participants. There would be no book, nor clinic, nor inspiration, without my people and the places we meet.

CONCEPTION

Albina Press, the only coffee shop open at six in the morning, seven days a week. My back-of-the-shop Genius Crew, especially my writer copilot, Charles Gillies. Also, Michael, Allison, Kyle, Aaron, Jescika, Christina. The darlings, Roxy and Pete and Sleeper Coffee. The Attic Institute and the authors who lifted up this doctor who loved to write: Brian Benson, Karen Karbo, Whitney Otto. The early-morning friends, the runners and dreamers: Kate Moore, Claire Teasdale, Molly Boyl, Faith Dawson. Fellow California nerd girl Gina Biehl, and the rest of the Vegas 8: Amy Lawrence, Trisha Highland, Kristy Olson, Keli Cronen, Karen Hansen, Shannon

Moran, Suzanne Cronen. My dear friend and luminous author, Apricot Irving.

GESTATION

In my literary agent, Lindsay Edgecombe, I found an Olympic coach, a diplomat, and a bulldog. She held, swaddled, nursed, rocked—did anything at any time to grow our vision to completion. I am forever indebted to Lauren Wein, my dreams-do-come-true editor, who believed that not only my story but also my grandmother's was worthy to tell. She held the squat bar through the impossible weaving of the past with the present and implored me to push even harder each time I thought we were done. To the entire crew at Avid Reader Press, especially Amy Guay, for insight and consistent support, and Rebecca Rodd with Levine Greenberg Rostan, who first read the manuscript and forwarded it to Lindsay—thank you. Alexis Gargagliano came in at the end and got us to the finish line. Nicky Taylor offered original edits years ago. To the island of Mallorca, Fibonacci café, Thomas' Bakeshop, Sóller SUP, Alice, Heather, Rosie, Jules, Costanza, Michelle, Jon Kristiansen—*mil gracias.*

STAGE 1: DILATION AND EFFACEMENT

The ones who are there for the expansion: Dr. Emmy Lawrason-Kobobel, with unconditional love, wisdom, and daily Marco Polos. Shawnee Shahroody Spitler, the OG bestie who loved me at twelve when few others did and has been there every day since. Kate Nason, my fairy godmother weaving connections and linen and words. TWFKAJR (Jennifer Malnick) with the earliest edits, the earliest friendship, and the most laughs. Adam Miller, the most gracious forever high school BF. Amy Duffy, my college game-changer who taught me what matters most. Angela Zachary, my cheerleader and full-heart-living inspiration. Leon Zachary, husband goals. Ali Mohajerani, my life sensei. Elie Mohajerani, my love sensei. Shams Mohajerani, the best of both worlds. Brian Patrolia, sheets in the shower and toothpaste caviar. Christine Salinas. Renee James. Johnette Johnson. Maura Hanlon. My Touro College of Osteopathic Medicine family: Drs. Bethany Engblom, Nadia Tereshchenko, Mary DiGiulio, Jason Steindler, Kimberlie Keller. You are all with me.

STAGE 2: EXPULSION

The team defines the experience. My hospital communities: Hartford Hospital, New Britain General, University of Connecticut, Asante Rogue Medical Center, Providence Hospital, Adventist Hospital, Legacy Mount Hood Medical Center. Every labor nurse and especially my closest allies on the unit: Cyndee Lacuna, Lorinda Schnackenberg, Alicia Manwiller, Alejandrina Felipe, Brooke Strande, Kelsi Wetz, Beth Burks, Nicole Craun, Jen Lange, Samantha Crowley, Kasey Hudson, Yoko Ackerman, Peggy Gwyn, Karina Gomez, Donna Clark, Katilin Ironside, Breyanna Freeman, Maureen Higgins. The Certified Nurse Midwives: Kirsten Gwynn, Shannon Thurston, Christin Trost, Haley Beeson, Sayre White, Julie Shiprack, Alison Spillane, Jessi Hargadine. The anesthesiologists, including my lifetime amigo Dr. Randall Ford. Drs. Winston Chang, Michelle Smith, Luke Parr, Andrew Smith. CRNA extraordinaire Mauri Traylor. The UConn Obstetrics and Gynecology Residency class of 2010: the most laughs, the most tears—Drs. Michael Hemphill, Stacy Slat, Caitlin Saint-Aubin, Natalie C. Webb, Stephanie Garozzo, Chris Nold, Cynthia Elis, Kristina Ericsson. My indefatigable boss, Dr. Karen Archabald. Also, Dr. Jennifer Lincoln for her tireless vision and activism. Everyone from Gresham Women's Healthcare, PC. My Oregon ob-gyn partners, my hearts: Drs. Sandi Collis, Kelly Carter, Anne Knudsen, Renee Goodreau, Edward Yanke, Diana Gill, Claudia Rojas, Audra Norris, Britta Ameel, Monica Venn, Michael Farber, Michael Traynor, Brooke Renard, Krissy Roesen, Greg Eilers, Anika Denali Luengo, Kathleen Wilder, Quang Nguyen, Alvin Nakamura, Lishiana Shaffer, Maryanne Garvie-Loveland, Deborah Taylor, Joy Anderson, Carissa Dames, Jonathan Freeman.

STAGE 3: DELIVERY OF THE PLACENTA

The afterbirth, sometimes effortless, sometimes the most intense. My mobile clinic family: Terra Presley, Laura Rojas—my sisters, my partners, my friends. Together, our vision of a magical space on wheels came to exist. You two are FemForward forever. Also, Devonne Lawrason for keeping us in line. Robyn Blatchford, our champion. Kimberly Roberts, Lauren Harris, Cindy Humiston, Victoria Blachly, Timothy Resch for business and legal. Our community partners: Black & Beyond the Binary Collective, Calcagno Pediatrics, Southwest Family Physicians, Seeding Justice. Our patients. Our patients. Our most extraordinary patients.

POSTPARTUM

The long days and longer nights. The doulas of daily life. John Esbeck, who poured love and wine through much of it. Bella and Sophia Esbeck, beautiful in and out. My gorgeous, gregarious Iranian family—Uncles Mansour, Saeed, Afshin, Armin, Mansour, Khoshnoud, Massoud, Bijan, Daryoush. Aunties Nargess, Marjan, Khojasteh, Shayesteh, Jila. The cousins: Halleh, Sarah, Joseph, Matt, Elise, Amir, Amir Ali, Amir Hossein, Nedda, Neggin, Nima, Sonia, Marisa, Layla, Sarah, Shabnam, Nassim, Mohammad Ali, Abdol Reza, Ali Reza, Hamid Reza, Afsaneh, Amin, Maisam, Payam, Milad, Sohail, Nahal, Nellie, Zahgros, and Keyhan. The nephews: Lincoln, Klae, Roan, Milan, Leon. The nieces: Ava, Lucy, Lilliana, Haleigh, Kaleigh, Devyn. The neighborhood: Isaiah, Asher, Sebastian, Stone, Skyla, Alma, Clara, Camila. The parents: Chad Honl and Isabel Toledo-Honl. Joni and Scott Sobel. Kara Busse and Juan Carlos Ordonez. The dynamic and wise supporting duo Izayah Jeffrey and John Underwood. The therapist who holds all the secrets, Amy Greenfield. Also with sorcery, Michael Deangelo. Playa de Barrio and the Goddesses: whale whisperer Katherina Audley; the yogis Kelli Jo Scott, Tarrell Kullaway, Erika Anderson, Nova Knutson, Eric Corbett; my teacher—Alison Alstrom.

FOREVER

My father, Dr. Khosrow Afsari, and his larger-than-life enthusiasm for medicine, his most earnest qualities, and his love that passed on to me. Dr. Mahshid Afsari, compassionate, beautiful child whisperer who is mother to everyone, making me the luckiest to call her mom. Keith Howard, with partnership, patience, and giving me the greatest gift of mama. Cornelia and Hugh Devlin, the generous, coolest in-laws. My angels, De and Marv Gaston, for believing I could be their granddaughter. Dr. Navid Madani, my second cousin sister, my matriarchal line, rocking chairs on porches forever. My sisses-in-law—Dr. Louisa Cammidge, Bertha Afsari, Elie Afsari—for giving me the other side of the story. My brother Michael for his love and his daughters. My big brother Peter for walking through this life directly by my side. My Bob, the middle brother, the most extra, for calling me every day and being the net that allows a girl to jump. And ultimately, the babies. My babies. Who grew their umbilical cords and then learned to run. Kai Khosrow Howard, Naiya Marie Howard—you are your own. And you are forever mine.

About the Author

MARY FARIBA AFSARI, DO, is a board-certified ob-gyn who founded FemForward Health in Portland, Oregon. She graduated from the University of Connecticut School of Medicine Obstetrics and Gynecology Residency Program and also holds an MS in health communication from Tufts University/Emerson College. *Labor: One Woman's Work* is her first book.

Avid Reader Press, an imprint of Simon & Schuster, is built on the idea that the most rewarding publishing has three common denominators: great books, published with intense focus, in true partnership. Thank you to the Avid Reader Press colleagues who collaborated on *Labor*, as well as to the hundreds of professionals in the Simon & Schuster advertising, audio, communications, design, ebook, finance, human resources, legal, marketing, operations, production, sales, supply chain, subsidiary rights, and warehouse departments whose invaluable support and expertise benefit every one of our titles.

Editorial
Lauren Wein, *VP and Editor-in-Chief*
Amy Guay, *Associate Editor*

Jacket Design
Alison Forner, *Senior Art Director*
Clay Smith, *Senior Designer*
Sydney Newman, *Art Associate*

Marketing
Meredith Vilarello, *VP and Associate Publisher*
Kayla Dee, *Associate Marketing Manager*
Katya Wiegmann, *Marketing and Publishing Assistant*

Production
Allison Green, *Managing Editor*
Hana Handzija, *Managing Editorial Assistant*
Jessica Chin, *Senior Manager of Copyediting*
Morgan Hart, *Senior Production Editor*
Allison Har-zvi, *Senior Production Manager*
Ruth Lee-Mui, *Interior Text Designer*
Briana Skerpan, *Desktop Compositor*
Cait Lamborne, *Ebook Developer*

Publicity
Rhina Garcia, *Senior Publicist*
Eva Kerins, *Publicity Assistant*

Subsidiary Rights
Paul O'Halloran, *VP and Director of Subsidiary Rights*
Fiona Sharp, *Subsidiary Rights Coordinator*